The
Millionaire
in the
Mirror

The Millionaire *in the* Mirror

HOW TO FIND YOUR PASSION AND MAKE A FORTUNE DOING IT—WITHOUT QUITTING YOUR DAY JOB

Gene Bedell

Collins

An Imprint of HarperCollinsPublishers

HarperCollins books may be purchased for educational, business, or sales promotional use. For information, please write: Special Markets Department, HarperCollins Publishers, 10 East 53rd Street, New York, NY 10022.

FIRST EDITION

Library of Congress Cataloging-in-Publication Data

Bedell, Gene.
    The millionaire in the mirror : how to find your passion and make a fortune doing it—without quitting your day job / Gene Bedell. —1st ed.
        p. cm.
    ISBN 978–0–06–147348–7
    1. Success in business 2. Career development. 3. Vocational guidance. 4. Quality of work life. I. Title.
HF5386.B355 2008
650.1—dc22

                                                    2007046518

08 09 10 11 12   OV/RRD   10 9 8 7 6 5 4 3 2 1

To Zoe and Zach:

Not everything in life is possible.
But love and Outstanding Success are.
Then all else will take care of itself.

The ladder of success doesn't care who climbs it.

Attributed to Frank Tyger

CONTENTS

Part II
Putting Strategies into Practice

INTRODUCTION

Outstanding Success

In this Introduction:

- What it means to be an Outstanding Success,
- How you can control your luck,
- Why hard work and sacrifice are overrated, and
- Why you're already talented enough to become an Outstanding Success.

> *If I could drop dead right now,*
> *I'd be the happiest man alive.*
>
> Samuel Goldwyn

ENOUGH MONEY TO CHANGE PEOPLE'S LIVES

It was a cold winter Sunday afternoon in Virginia—raining, gloomy—a day to spend indoors, surrounded by sleeping wet-smelling dogs. With nothing better to do, I decided finally to clean out my old files and books, which grow in my basement like barnacles on the bottom of a boat. I went downstairs with a large plastic trash bag and good intentions.

And there they were—my tax records for every year of my life since I started paying taxes. Hmmm. That was the end of my good intentions. I decided instead to add up the amount of money I'd earned since I began my career. Then I adjusted the amounts for inflation to see what it all came to in today's dollars.

The total wasn't in Bill Gates or Warren Buffett territory, but it still seemed like a lot of money. A half hour of research on the Internet, and I learned I'd earned more than ten times the amount earned by the average household during the same period. Less than 1% of all United States households earned more. Assuming an inflation rate of 3.5%, those just starting their careers today would have to earn $42 million over the course of forty years to be in the top 1%. This amount won't put them among the idle rich, but it's more than enough to change most people's lives. And I had done it without sacrifice to my family and personal life. It has been, at least most of the time, a hoot.

Money has never been the dominant driving force in my life, so my reaction to seeing how much I earned was, "Can you imagine that? How on earth did I get the world to pay me so much more money than it paid nearly everyone else?"

My original goal was simply to give my college-age children more Dad-advice they didn't really want to listen to. That's how I started work on this book. I was looking for a simple answer to give my children to a seemingly simple question: what is it that makes some people happier and more successful in their work than others? But the search took over my life, as for two years I wound up studying happiness and financial success at work, a magic combination I call Outstanding Success.

Just looking at earning and happiness, however, wasn't enough. My daughter was headed to the public sector, where success is measured less by your earnings and more by the influence you have in your chosen field. So I expanded the definition of Outstanding Success to include being happy in your work and achieving a position that allows you to be among the most influential people in your field. I began by studying my career, then the careers of ten people I knew well who had achieved Outstanding Success, then the careers of people I coached, most of whom came to me because they had not achieved Outstanding Success.

Nothing came out as I expected.

Outstanding Success is a career's best prize—outstanding earnings or influence in your field combined with outstanding happiness. If you're going to spend forty years of your life working anyway, this is what you should be working for.

But is how successful you become really in your power, or is it just a matter of good luck, innate talent, and the willingness to work so hard you destroy your personal life? We need to answer this question before looking for Outstanding Success strategies, because if the secrets to Outstanding Success are luck, talent, and hard work, you don't need a book to succeed. You need good fortune, good genes, and a willingness to suffer and sacrifice.

YOU SET THE GAME

Face it, success depends at least partially on good luck. But good luck comes into play only after you've set the game.

Say you write the word "Success" on five sides of a six-sided die and "Failure" on the sixth. You've set the probability of Success appearing when you throw the die at five out of six and Failure at one in six. Once you've painted the sides, either on a real die or metaphorically on the die of life, the rest is out of your hands. You establish the probabilities, and then luck takes over. You're the one who determines which plays the bigger role—you or luck. You set the game.

Gary was the successful head of marketing and sales of a midsize technology company. He was earning good money and having fun traveling around the world, managing his empire and closing sales. No problem. Except that Gary saw that the real fun, influence, and earnings came from being the CEO. And for a number of reasons that aren't important to this story, this wasn't likely to happen at his current company. His die had "Success" written on only one of the six sides.

It's no easy decision to take a winning hand and throw it in (to mix gambling metaphors), but Gary saw that if he was serious about moving from "good money" to being a top 1% earner, he had to change the game. So he left his secure, comfortable position with an established company headquartered in the South. He took a CEO job with a struggling three-year-old company in Minnesota (state motto: Brrrrr) at less than half his former earnings but with a significant equity stake.

Of course it could have turned out to be a bad bet. But in fact, in three years Gary's equity stake was worth nearly $10 million. He had changed his odds of success and good luck came his way.

So, are people who have achieved Outstanding Success lucky? Of course they are. If you look more deeply, however, you'll find that in nearly every case they were lucky because they managed themselves into a position where they were more likely to be lucky. The strategies for achieving Outstanding Success do not deny the role of good fortune. Quite the contrary. What they do is tilt the odds in your favor by maximizing the chances that you will achieve Outstanding Success, if not in a single throw of the "Success" die, then after repeated throws.

Even if you're in the middle of your career and you haven't managed your career so that "Success" is painted on enough sides of your die, it's probably not too late to change things. Sure, luck will still be involved, but like the twentysomething just starting out, you can swing the probabilities more in your favor.

So let's neither obsess about luck, nor make light of its role in life. It will be a factor in your career, but bad luck is rarely a good excuse for failure to achieve Outstanding Success. If you manage your career properly and don't let a failure or two get you down, good enough luck will eventually come your way.

HARD WORK IS OVERRATED

What does it even mean to work hard today? For our fore-bears, work meant physical labor, and hours of work per day translated into acres of fields plowed or number of sheep sheared, mastodons killed, pounds of butter churned, cords of firewood chopped. For our ancestors there was a direct relationship between how hard they worked, the value they produced, and the number of calories they burned producing it. They didn't spend time in endless meetings in the barn or the cave, traveling an entire day in an ox cart for a one-hour meeting with a prospect, chang-ing the fonts on PowerPoint presentations that were for-gotten as soon as the Pilgrims left the public square, or doing other "work" that didn't produce concrete results. Nor did they use work time to chat around the well, shop online, or surf the Web.

Today, for managers and knowledge workers, there is frequently no direct relationship between how long they work and useful results. When you're doing the wrong things, working long hours is a waste of time and energy. You may be wearing an Armani suit and sincere shoes, burning the midnight oil, living on airplanes, and spend-ing your time in meetings with big-time muckety-mucks, but you might as well be staring out the window, counting out-of-state license plates.

Of course sometimes hard work is necessary in re-sponse to a special pressure or need—but not always and forever. For the most part, when you're doing the right things, and only the right things, you won't have to work exceptionally long hours as a matter of course and sacri-fice the rest of what's important in your life. Eight good hours a day, maybe a little more from time to time, will usually do it.

But not always.

It doesn't matter how good you are or how smart you work, you cannot become a partner in a major big-city law firm, a managing director at one of the country's largest investment banks, or a key software developer at a struggling high-tech start-up company and be home for dinner with the kids at five thirty every night.

These and similar organizations place extreme demands on the people who work for them, sometimes of necessity and sometimes as a result of a misguided culture. Working for such organizations can be the most fun you'll ever have at work or the worst experience of your life. Sometimes both at different times.

I have worked on Wall Street, for Midwest manufacturing firms, for struggling high-tech start-ups, and in my own businesses. I have watched closely the careers of people who live to work and people who work to live, people who sacrifice their family lives for career success and people who wouldn't miss their kids' Little League games or dance recitals even if it meant leaving dinner with the firm's biggest client in the middle of the shrimp cocktail.

My observation is that the idea of working hard is overrated. The fact is, some successful people work hard and some don't. Some not-so-successful people don't work hard, but many others do. The only thing that's certain about working hard is that no one will stop you. They may not award you appropriately, but they'll let you work till you drop. It was not how hard people worked that determined whether they were successful, it was what they worked on and how they worked when they worked.

Justin worked for a rapidly growing company in a high-tech industry. The company's staff were highly motivated young people caught up in the excitement of building a company they thought could "change the world" and earn them a fortune in the process. The average age of the employees was less than thirty, and for most of them, their life was their work. It was not unusual to find systems engineers sleeping in their offices, showering in the gym, and spending days at a time without going home.

But this wasn't for Justin. Although he was as motivated, excited, and ambitious as everyone else, staying in top physical condition through running, biking, lifting weights, and playing tennis was a top priority. As were his four children.

Every day Justin would arrive at the gym or the tennis courts by 5:00 a.m. so he could work out before heading to work. Every day he was in the office, he'd run or bike during his lunch hour, almost always with colleagues from work. It wasn't unusual for runs or bike rides to turn into hour-long business discussions that would ordinarily have taken place with everyone sitting around a conference room, drinking coffee or Diet Coke. People knew that if you wanted Justin's undivided attention, you ran or biked with him at noontime, and that he'd always match his pace to one comfortable for you.

When Justin traveled on business, he'd stay at hotels that were a few miles from a good gym. He'd rise early, run to the gym, work out, run back to the hotel, shower, and be ready for business with everyone else. When he wasn't traveling, he was on the train heading home no later than six o'clock, in time for dinner with his family.

But when he was at work, he was at work. Studies repeatedly document that people waste, on average, 40% of the time they spend at work, and Justin could see it happening even in his high-energy company. He would tell me, "Don't listen to what people tell you is important to them. Watch what they do. If someone says they really want to get into shape, but they spend their lunchtime eating and socializing, it's the eating and socializing that's important. If they say they want to spend more time with their family, but they waste two hours a day at work or watching television, maybe in their hearts they really don't want to spend more time with their family."

Justin went on to become the CEO of several companies without ever abandoning his exercise routine. He also stayed closely involved with his children, one of whom had special needs requiring extra time and attention. He was able to do this, in part, because he knew what he wanted from work and what was important to him outside work. He didn't waste time kibitzing at the office, doing crossword puzzles during his commute, or watching TV in the evenings. He knew what mattered, and very simply, he focused on what mattered and only on what mattered.

Know that, for most of us, how hard we work is a personal choice. I've found happiness living between the two extremes of living to work and working to live, but to each his own. Select a position on this spectrum of the work-life continuum based on your personality, predilections, and interests, and choose where you work accordingly. With some notable exceptions, you *can* become an Outstanding Success without sacrificing the rest of your life. In the end, how hard you work isn't the deciding factor among Outstanding Success, mediocrity, and outright career failure. Decide how much time you're willing to devote to your work, choose your career path appropriately, and stop whining about how hard you work.

SURPRISINGLY, YOU'RE TALENTED ENOUGH

Could it be that, as in professional sports, entertainment, and the arts, the secret of achieving Outstanding Success is talent? Surprisingly, it's not, something I began to understand, at first to my dismay and later to my delight, after I carefully analyzed my own talents.

I say "carefully analyzed" because, as it turns out, it's not as easy to analyze yourself as you might think. Consider a study that asked men to rate their natural athletic abilities by comparing themselves with the rest of the population. Ninety percent of the men studied placed themselves in the top 10%. Women, I am sure, will not find this mass male delusion surprising, as most have ample personal experience with men who rate themselves *well* above average in skills more intimate than athletics, if you catch my drift.

But this tendency to see ourselves as far more skilled than we are is not limited to men. Similar studies found that 80% of drivers put themselves in the top 30% in driving ability, and 60% of high school students rank themselves among the top 10% in their ability to get along with others. We live in a Lake Wobegon world, where everyone is above average.

No one is immune from this perception-reality disconnect, including college students, stock market analysts, and (uh-oh) business managers and CEOs. Scarier still, another study, done by Cornell scientists Justin Kruger and David Dunning, "Unskilled and Unaware of It: How Difficulties in Recognizing One's Own Incompetence Lead to Inflated Self-Awareness,"* found that one char-

---

* *Journal of Personality and Social Psychology* 77:6 (1999):1121–1134.

acteristic of incompetent people is that they are incapable of knowing they are incompetent!

I love these studies because they show not only how much our self-perceptions are out of touch with reality, but also how clueless we are to the fact that we're out of touch with reality. But they made me worry that I would have an ego bias that would taint whatever conclusions I came up with when I analyzed my own talents. I had to protect myself from my egocentric self.

Knowing the extent to which people overstate their talents, I decided to be especially careful to do a realistic inventory to see what it is I'm so good at that I've had the success I've had. I stepped outside myself and did what I think is an objective, critical reality check. No varnish, no delusions, no wishful thinking. If I couldn't find clear, indisputable evidence of a particular personal strength or skill, I assumed I most likely didn't have it.

Guess what? I couldn't find evidence of anything I was especially good at. All around me I saw people who are better than I am at everything that's important in business— selling, marketing, managing and dealing with people, planning, technology, public speaking. And not just the top people in business; even average people in business turn out to be about as good at just about everything.

Don't get me wrong. I wasn't like Dilbert's goofball, pointy-haired boss, getting by on the work and talent of all the hapless Dilberts in the world. I was as good as most people at most things that are important in business. And that's the point—I was as good as most people but not noticeably better. It was reality dope-slapping me on the side of the head, and it changed entirely the way I thought about career success.

But wait. Maybe the cause of my success is not some

special talent, but simply superior intellect. I wish. In the strict sense of the word, when it comes to intelligence, I'm not an average person, because an average person has an IQ of slightly over 100. While I don't know what my IQ is, to make it through college mine is undoubtedly higher than average. But I doubt it's significantly higher than the IQ of the average engineering college graduate. *I'm an average above-average person*—smart enough to get through college but certainly not the smartest guy in the class. In other words, chances are I'm pretty much like you.

AVERAGE ABOVE-AVERAGE PEOPLE

It would be interesting but not useful if achieving Outstanding Success without being outstanding was unique to me. I could just have been plain lucky, in the right place at the right time. Or had some unique combination of ordinary skills that fortuitously resulted in extraordinary achievement. So I looked around me for other people who had achieved Outstanding Success.

Of course, some people who have achieved Outstanding Success have Ivy League educations, Harvard MBAs, or family connections. But as it turns out, most do not. Moreover, with each passing decade, fewer and fewer successful people come from the Ivy League. In 1980, 23% of large company CEOs had bachelor's degrees from an Ivy League school. That had dropped to 19% by 1990 and to 10% by 2005.

Typical are ten people I know, seven men and three women. All have worked in business their entire careers, and all have achieved Outstanding Success. They all have a net worth between $10 million and more than $100 million, every dollar of which they earned entirely through their own efforts.

What I found most remarkable was that, with the exception of having achieved Outstanding Success, none is in any way remarkable. All are above average in intelligence, but no more so than the people they work with and most likely no more so than this book's readers. The average SAT scores for the group was around 1150 (out of the maximum 1600 possible under the old SAT grading system), with one actually scoring as low as the 900s. None went to an Ivy League or big-name school, and none came from a family with money or influence. Only three have MBAs (none from a prestigious business school), and one has less than a year of college. Yet they all greatly outperformed their peers, often hard-working, brilliant people, many of whom attended better schools.

Ben is one of the more interesting cases of Outstanding Success I know because his mercurial, almost bipolar personality has resulted in repeated career dislocations. If you were to graph the careers of most people who achieve Outstanding Success, you'd see a relatively smooth graph that begins with upward progress much like everyone else's in the very early years. Then, somewhere between five and ten years into the career, the graph line of the Outstandingly Successful person begins a steep climb that becomes increasingly steeper with time, while the graph line of the average career levels out. With the exception of an occasional setback, however, the graph line of the Outstanding Success would move continually upward.

But that's not what you would see looking at Ben's career graph line. You'd see a distinct and erratic sawtooth pattern of rapid climbs tracking those of other Outstanding Successes, but followed by precipitous drops and restarts. More often than not, the drops were self-inflicted career dislocations or setbacks resulting from Ben's interesting but somewhat volatile personality.

Nevertheless, for whatever the reason, the result was that Ben was repeatedly put into a position where he was starting over, if not at the very beginning of his career, at the very beginning of climbs that separate those who achieve Outstanding Success from everyone else. Yet he succeeded repeatedly—providing a one-man set of observations for a study in Outstanding Success.

What can we learn from Ben? He grew up in a two-parent home, but one that suffered frequent economic distress, and he received no career guidance from his struggling parents. He is as intelligent as most intelligent people I know, but for some reason he scored lower on the SATs than anyone else I've worked with. He earned bachelor's and master's degrees, graduating high in his class but from decidedly undistinguished schools. He certainly didn't begin his career with connections or social advantage. Yet despite the lack of special talents, education, or privilege, he has repeatedly put himself on track to achieve Outstanding Success, and over the course of his career has in fact achieved it.

From the standpoint of my study of Outstanding Success, Ben is almost a textbook example of an average above-average person with no special advantages who has been able to succeed repeatedly—not due to special luck or talent, but though Outstanding Success behavior.

FOR YOU AND ME, BEHAVIOR, NOT TALENT, DETERMINES SUCCESS

Having determined that it wasn't luck, hard work, or talent that separated average above-average people who achieve

Outstanding Success from all the rest of the average above-average people, the natural question was, what was it? I was looking for much more than good career hygiene—habits and practices that should be part of everyone's work life but don't necessarily lead to Outstanding Success. I'd read too many books by success coaches, consultants, motivational speakers, and retired executives who spouted management clichés like "Pick good people and get out of their way," or "Stay in touch with the customer," or "Be a good listener," or "Do what you love." Groan.

You can't dispute the righteousness of these maxims. But these are the kind of things both successful and not-so-successful people do. If this is what I told my children, they'd listen intently for as long as it took them to escape from the room, at which point they'd immediately forget whatever it was I'd said.

I found seven strategies shared by people who achieve Outstanding Success in business careers, strategies that are generally *not* followed by people who do not achieve Outstanding Success. Along the way, I discussed these strategies with people with careers in the public sector—teaching, government, the military, law enforcement—and other not-for-profit organizations. Although the potential for high earnings was different in these careers, if your goal is to achieve Outstanding Success, the career strategies are the same.

I didn't expect to find that it is ordinary behavior and not outstanding talent that leads to Outstanding Success in the careers most of us follow. What I found is counterintuitive because we have come to associate success with talent, a misconception I suspect comes from a few highly visible, highly publicized career paths for which talent is in fact a prerequisite for success. These high-talent careers dominate the news and, consequently, our consciousness. But while we may all secretly fantasize about a career in professional sports, entertainment, or the arts, and some of us see ourselves as Supreme Court justices or winning a Nobel Prize, few of us follow these paths. Instead, *most of us have careers where it is our behavior, and not our talent, that is most instrumental in determining our success.*

Oversimplifying somewhat, most careers require that we *do* things, not that we perform, discover, create, or entertain. And what we have to do is just not that difficult. Compare accounting, selling, programming, managing, running a factory, and other organization stuff to tackling an NFL fullback, singing at the Metropolitan Opera, or decoding the human genome, and you get the idea. Unlike playing a Mozart concerto to a packed house at Carnegie Hall or hitting a tee shot on the back nine on the Sunday of the Masters, most of what has to be done in our careers is something most average college-educated people can learn once they apply themselves.

So stop worrying about whether you're talented enough to become an Outstanding Success. Most likely you are, if for no other reason than it just doesn't take that much talent.

A CAREER OPERATING MANUAL

This book is an operating manual for managing your career. It is based on the fundamental idea that *ordinary people have the power to achieve financial success and happiness in their work if they take control and personally manage their careers.* It has a simple purpose—to help you achieve Outstanding Success.

Part I, chapters I through 7, discusses the seven strategies essential for achieving Outstanding Success in your career. They provide the underlying principles for managing your career. Following the strategies won't guarantee you'll join Bill Gates as one of the world's wealthiest and most influential people, but it will greatly improve your chance of both loving your work and becoming at least moderately wealthy and influential.

Part II moves from the theory of achieving Outstanding Success to actually doing it. Chapter 8 provides guidelines for implementing the seven Outstanding Success strategies without the help of a career coach. Chapter 9 addresses the problems you'll face working with dysfunctional organizations or with dysfunctional people. Chapter 10 helps you restart your career on a more productive track if you're stuck in an eddy. Chapter 11 presents a realistic view of the major business alternatives—working for yourself as an entrepreneur, starting a venture capital—backed business, buying a franchise, or working for a business you don't own and control. Lastly, chapter 12 answers some important questions I suspect you'll have after you finish reading the first eleven chapters.

NO NASTY TRICKS

The focus on Outstanding Success, and particularly on money and influence, may conjure up visions of cutthroat competition and even marginally ethical behavior as you claw your way to the top. Forget it.

There are no nasty tricks involved here, no organizational politics, no Machiavellian scheming. And unlike many books directed to helping people become happy and successful, *The Millionaire in the Mirror* does not discourage you from working for large organizations or for companies you don't own and control. Nor does it promote trying to become financially independent through get-rich-quick schemes or by opting out of a conventional career to get away from a job that's not leading anywhere.

Don't get me wrong. It's okay not to like your job and to be unhappy with your career at the moment. You can do something about that without chucking it all and moving to Vermont to raise free-range chickens. But if you want to make the most of the opportunities available to you and achieve Outstanding Success, you must manage your career carefully.

Which is why you need a career operating manual.

PART I

OUTSTANDING

SUCCESS

STRATEGIES

*Success is a science; if you have the conditions,
you get the result.*

Oscar Wilde

CHAPTER 1

OUTSTANDING SUCCESS STRATEGY #1

Become a Heat-Seeking Missile

In this chapter:

- Leaving the past behind,
- Becoming a Heat-Seeking Missile and not a Searcher, Drifter, or one of the Forlorn, and
- Locking onto a career target.

> *To reach a port, we must sail—*
> *Sail, not tie at anchor—*
> *Sail, not drift.*
>
> FRANKLIN ROOSEVELT

"YESTERDAY" IS JUST THE TITLE OF A BEATLES SONG

If you follow the directions in the operating manual that comes with your new coffeemaker or car, you can expect to have a predictable, relatively trouble-free experience. If you follow the directions in this career operating manual, on the other hand, it's unlikely your career will be as predictable and trouble free as your coffeemaker experience.

With a career, even if you do everything right and achieve Outstanding Success, there undoubtedly will be plenty of surprises and a few disappointments along the way. Moreover, even if you follow this book's advice to the letter, it's almost inevitable that you'll still make a few mistakes you'll have to recover from.

There's another way a career operating manual differs from other operating manuals. When we open the box of a new coffeemaker or take delivery on a new car, the first thing we do is sit down and read the operating manual. Careers don't work that way.

While it's possible you're reading this before you start out on a new career, it's more likely you're somewhere between early in your career to twenty to thirty years into it. You've made a lot of choices along the way—some good, some not so good. It's a little like driving your new car for fifty thousand miles before reading the owner's manual for the first time and learning you should have changed the oil every five thousand miles. Oops.

But wherever you are in your career and whatever choices you've made, there's an undeniable fact that holds for everyone: *there's nothing we can do about the past.* And it is with this absolute truth in mind that you should read the book's seven strategies.

For example, in this chapter, you will read about four distinctly different types of people:

• Heat-Seeking Missiles

• Searchers

• Drifters

• The Forlorn

You must spend most of your career as a Heat-Seeking Missile if you hope to achieve Outstanding Success. Fine, but what if you're well into your career and have spent very little of it as a Heat-Seeking Missile? You get to slap your forehead once and maybe say to yourself, "I wish I'd known this earlier."

That's it for the past. Put it behind you. "Yesterday" is just the title of a Beatles song. Don't rue past decisions. Don't beat yourself up or compare yourself with others. From this point on, you need to forget the past and accept that you are where you are, because it is only what you do from this point forward that will change your career trajectory.

But even if you're just starting out in your career and you follow every strategy to the letter, don't expect your journey to be an uninterrupted series of ups. Even if everything goes perfectly, you still have to deal with the most unpredictable element in your formula for career success and personal happiness—you.

It may take you years to discover what stirs your passions and makes you happy. Or you may be happy and successful for years and wake up one morning to suddenly find you need a change—maybe even a big change.

So your journey to Outstanding Success may have many bumps and potholes, a few downs along with the ups. We're talking reality here, not some fantasy career. In the real world, even people who achieve Outstanding Success occasionally go through some bad spells. And people who have had years or even decades of bad spells can turn things around and move toward achieving Outstanding Success.

So don't become discouraged if you haven't always made the best career decisions or if you don't seem to be headed in the direction of Outstanding Success. Today is soon enough to start following the seven strategies if for no other reason than you can't start any sooner. And the first thing to do if you're a Drifter, a Searcher, or one of the Forlorn is to become a Heat-Seeking Missile.

HEAT-SEEKING MISSILES

Heat-Seeking Missiles have career targets imprinted in their minds, have mapped these targets and aspirations into concrete short- and medium-term goals, and they manage their careers *day to day* in a way that leads to achieving these goals. They are locked onto a career target and are not influenced by organizational chaff that can throw them off course—short-term earnings, fancy job titles, big offices, training, management responsibilities, comfort, or security. If their job isn't contributing to increasing their career value and moving them toward their career objective, they change jobs.

George was twenty-eight when one of the country's top investment banks recruited him to build a computing and quantitative analysis group to support the company's two primary businesses—corporate finance and securities trading. He was an engineer without an MBA or a degree from any of the four Ivy League schools this investment bank recruited from, and he would not ordinarily have been able to land a job with this prestigious Wall Street firm. But this was just as quantitative analysis was becoming a dominant force in finance, so the bank's partners felt they needed someone with a much different background—one grounded in computing and math. It was a unique opportunity for George to become part of one of the most influential and wealthy firms in financial services.

George's work was intellectually interesting, and his colleagues smart, supportive, and friendly. Everyone considered George's performance to be outstanding, and his earnings doubled in the first two years. He was on his way.

But despite being happy with his work, company, success, colleagues, and earnings growth, George sensed he was drifting. His objective was to become a senior officer in a major company, and what he was doing wouldn't lead him in that direction. It would, in fact, just lead him to do more of what he was already doing. Although his work was interesting and lucrative, it was not consistent with his career objectives. To the astonishment and consternation of his company's management, George chose to leave the bank after just two years to accept a lower-paying job in a less prestigious company. He made the decision because the new job would more likely lead to a meaningful senior management position in a major business.

George was a Heat-Seeking Missile, and he stayed on target despite the distraction of good pay, ego stroking, and interesting work. Eighteen months after joining his

new firm, he was promoted to vice president and shortly
after that to group vice president running the company's
largest operating business.

George was in his twenties when he made this move, but
Heat-Seeking Missiles come in all ages. Whenever a CEO
retires, it's almost inevitable that two things follow. First,
of course, someone is chosen to become the new CEO. But
the second thing to happen shortly thereafter is the an-
nouncement that the senior executive who was in line for
the CEO's job but did not get it is leaving the company.

The executive who failed to get the CEO job leaves even
though he may have been with the company for years and
is in a powerful, high-prestige, secure job, earning millions in compensation. He leaves because he is a Heat-
Seeking Missile whose goal is to become CEO. When he
finally knows he will not achieve that goal at the organization he's with, he leaves to join an organization where he
can achieve it.

It doesn't matter that he's leaving friends and associates
he's worked with for years, even decades, or that he might
have to move his family to a new region of the country, or
that he will be working in a new and unknown work environment with a much higher chance of failure. Executive
recruiters know that people destined to achieve Outstanding Success operate this way, and they are on the phone
offering the spurned executive new opportunities before
the ink dries on the *Wall Street Journal*'s blurb announcing
the new CEO.

SEARCHERS

Searchers are people who know they want to achieve something in their careers but don't know what it is. But not knowing what you want from your career is not enough to make you a Searcher. To be a Searcher, you must be actively searching for an end goal.

It's not a bad thing to be a Searcher; I have been one at numerous times in my career. It becomes a problem only if you spend too much time searching and too little time as a Heat-Seeking Missile.

Many young people are Searchers at the beginning of their careers. They take transition jobs in the hope that with the passage of time and the accumulation of experiences, inspiration will follow. They may teach for a year or they may join the armed services, consulting or accounting firms, or the Peace Corps. Or they may work as junior analysts or in gofer jobs on Wall Street or in professional firms, fully knowing they do not intend a career in these areas. Others hop from job to job, doing personal telemetry checks at each to see how they feel while assessing how good they are at whatever they're doing.

Whatever their searching strategy, they're uncommitted workers who are job dating, playing the field while they wait for the right career goal to come along. This is all good, as long as the Searcher knows her objective is to find a career direction that arouses interest and passion so she can lock onto it like a Heat-Seeking Missile.

I have met many Searchers among my daughter's friends, serious-minded, driven people who were just entering the workforce from college. Most know many things they do *not* want to do, but few have any positive idea where they want the forty-plus years of their working lives to take them.

One friend is committed to joining the army following graduation. When I asked if he intended the armed services to be his career, his response was that he doubted it, but he didn't know. He'd decide after a few years; maybe he'd stay in the military or maybe he'd go to law school. Or maybe something else. He just had not yet figured out where he was heading, but he has committed to exploring different possibilities.

Other Searchers are in midcareer but going through a transition. At one point they may have known what they wanted in their careers and committed themselves to achieving it. But then something happened. As a result of changes in their chosen field, the organization they work for, or their personal lives, they lost interest in the direction they were headed.

Matt was an attorney working toward a partnership in a New York City law firm. This is an arduous eight-year journey that requires such a complete commitment to the law and to the law firm and its clients that any semblance of work-life balance is impossible. It extracts a heavy sacrifice from the personal lives of those who choose this career path. Although he was successful in his job and ostensibly on a partnership track, six years into his career with the law firm Matt came to realize he lacked the one thing most necessary to make the sacrifice worthwhile—a love of the law.

Many big-city law firm associates experience similar career turmoil four to eight years into their careers. (The turnover among associates in New York City law firms can be as high as 36%.) Sometimes this happens because, like Matt, they discover that the area of the law they work in fails to interest them any longer, and sometimes because the aspiring lawyers feel the personal sacrifices and the price paid by their families are not worth the prize. Often it's simply because they gradually accept the reality that their firm is not going to make them a partner.

Typically, as in Matt's case, the associate then becomes a midcareer Searcher. The burning questions are, What do I want from my career? How do I want to spend my working life? Some give up on the idea of Outstanding Success entirely and drift along in less demanding jobs for the next ten or twenty years. They have respectable jobs and earn a good living, but never become as influential or financially successful as they'd envisioned.

Matt refused to drift or settle. He just wanted work that was more in tune with his interests. He'd always had a non-lawyer-like passion for technology, so he left his high-status general practice law firm and joined a specialty firm where he could focus on patent law, concentrating his energies on computing technology. Although his new career direction was less prestigious and financially less rewarding than his previous career path, twenty years later he's a recognized expert in his field, a top 1% earner, and perhaps most importantly, he loves going to work every morning.

DRIFTERS

Drifters are gainfully employed and may make "good money," work with amicable colleagues, have a pretty good time at work, and do not dislike what they do. Things are going fine, or at least not too badly, so there's no pressure to spend a lot of time and energy thinking through the big career picture. Besides, it's tough enough dealing with today without worrying about twenty years from today.

The prevailing Drifter attitude is, Hey, I'm good at what I do, and no matter what happens, there will always be a demand for people like me. Right? Right? Unfortunately, the answer to that question, and it doesn't matter what you do for a living, is usually no.

Interesting work, comfortable circumstances, good pay, and congenial colleagues are the deadly combination that produces Drifters. How, you might wonder, can anyone worry about this, when this is what most people look for in a job? But these people are wrong. *These job characteristics are the byproduct of Outstanding Success. But by themselves, they are a career death trap if they mask the fact that the job that provides them isn't leading you specifically where you want to be heading.*

My wife, daughter, and I were having dinner at a local pub. It was late, only a few people were still there, and I could overhear the conversation among the people at a nearby table. They were a couple in their early twenties having dinner with the husband's parents, and the son was proudly describing his new job. I shamelessly admit I listened in on their conversation with rapt attention as my wife and daughter pretended not to know me.

After just two or three minutes I got a clear picture of this man's job and where it could lead him, and it was not a happy place. I wanted to go over to his table, grab him by his metaphorical lapels (he was wearing a T-shirt), shake him, and scream, "No, no, no. You're screwing up! They're paying you $80,000 a year, and you think you're doing great. But I can tell from two tables away that you're in a dead-end job, your company is just using you up, and in a few years you're going to find yourself heading for the career trash heap piled high with smart, hard-working, unhappy people wondering what they did wrong. You've got to change your approach to work right now or you're toast."

Knowing what it takes to keep my marriage intact and my daughter from getting me committed, I bit my tongue, drank my beer, and was a little sad. Sad because I knew that in five years or so, when someone asked this person, "So how're you doing?" he'd answer, "Not bad, keeping busy, can't complain, pretty good considering." Or something along the lines of what people say who live lives of quiet desperation.

How could I know so quickly that the man at the other table was headed for trouble? Simple—his conversation centered largely on the accoutrements of being employed: the pay, vacations and holidays, the Friday afternoon parties, the fraternal atmosphere, even the chance to earn a sabbatical. But when he talked about what he actually did, he described a job where he was just one of a large group of helper bees doing work that had to be done for his company to succeed, but that, while interesting, didn't provide him an opportunity to distinguish himself. He was happy, having fun, and making good money but all the while drifting down a dead-end career track.

This phenomenon of the happy Drifter is distressingly common because it is easy to become a Drifter during the important ten to fifteen early years of what seems to be a promising career. You graduate from college and land your first real career job. Overnight you go from being a cash-constrained student to having a job that pays as much money in a month as you've had in any year.

Compared with school, a career life can be a walk in the

park—no constant testing, term papers, required readings, or Spanish verb conjugations to memorize. Sure, things are expected of you and you face occasional deadlines, but the relentless week-to-week short-interval scrutiny is gone. Life is good, even if you're putting in the hours.

Life is also much different. Instead of a world centered on earning good grades, getting into college or graduate school, or finishing a degree, it's focused on organizational goals like building systems, winning sales, producing products, teaching high school English, or any one of the millions of other things organizations do. This organization-centered focus disrupts the previously reliable relationship between the passage of time and your career value.

While you were in school, before your career began, just getting a year older and making it to the next grade level increased your personal career value, even if you hadn't chosen a career yet. This growth by sheer existence is something we all become accustomed to and take for granted during sixteen or more years of school. Then, on the day you leave school, the reliable link between the passage of time and the increase in your personal growth is no longer assured. Months, years, and even decades can pass with remarkably little personal growth. You drift for years without knowing you're drifting.

Drifters are like bottles floating on the ocean, going wherever the current takes them. Occasionally the current takes Drifters to fine places in their careers, and occasionally it washes them ashore. But if they allow themselves to drift too long, somewhere in their thirties to forties Drifters transmogrify into the Forlorn. It's a transition welcomed only by divorce lawyers and car dealers who sell red convertible sports cars to people trying to find some joy in their lives.

THE FORLORN

The Forlorn are the cannon fodder of middle management—experienced, competent people who do much of the repetitive, hard, and often boring work in Career World. But sadly, they are rewarded only with the opportunity to do more repetitive, hard, or boring work. They may be doing jobs that they enjoyed initially in accounting, teaching, sales, police work, law, publishing, financial services, manufacturing, engineering, administration, health care, government, or social services. But sometime between five and twenty years, their personal growth stopped and burnout or malaise set in.

They are important to the functioning of whatever organization they work for, but except for their immediate usefulness, they have largely been abandoned and show signs of neglect. They suffer pay raises that barely keep pace with inflation, they no longer receive promotions that bring meaningful increases in responsibility and influence, they report to younger colleagues, and are far, far out of the loop.

The Forlorn are hypersensitive to organizational changes, restructurings, and mergers and acquisitions. Any one of these events can wipe out an entire Forlorn colony, leaving behind no trace of its former existence except a sea of empty offices and cubicles with metaphorical wisps of smoke rising from desk chairs where middle managers once sat. At best, the Forlorn face a mediocre last half or even last two-thirds of their careers. And they have absolutely no idea how this all happened to them or what to do about it.

This is not abstract theory. A study of U.S. workers between the ages of thirty-five and fifty-four found that *two-thirds were not energized by their jobs, more than a third felt they were in dead-end jobs, and more than half felt no passion for their work*. Mid-career professionals had the lowest satisfaction rates with their bosses and the least confidence in top management. Where to go, what to do, is this all there is, are the tormenting questions. The result is personal frustration and a sense that the world is passing them by. And it is.

This is a feeling not yet shared by Searchers and Drifters. But all Searchers and Drifters are in danger of becoming the Forlorn if they wait too long to commit to a career goal and build the personal career value that will take them there.

NOW COMES THE HARD PART

It's fine to be a Searcher for a while, even for periods later in your career as you gain or regain your bearings and better understand your options. You can even be a Drifter for short periods if something in your personal life makes it difficult for you to make the career changes necessary to stay on target. But if you're a Searcher, you must eventually end your search. If you are a Drifter, you must stop drifting before it's too late. If you are one of the Forlorn, you must become unstuck. (More about how to become unstuck in chapter 10.)

To achieve Outstanding Success, you must spend most of your career as a Heat-Seeking Missile, which means you must commit to a career objective and lock onto it with single-minded purpose. It's the first strategy for achieving Outstanding Success, and it doesn't require talent, an Ivy League education, or a 140 IQ. All you have to do is manage your career so you direct all your energy and time to accomplishing a specific career objective.

It's not, however, as easy as it sounds.

The first thing you have to do to become a Heat-Seeking Missile is a snap, or so it would seem—decide what you want in life. Wealth, happiness, health, successful children, run your own business, be a Fortune 100 CEO, retire at forty, change the world, climb Mount Everest, own a Ferrari, become a rock god. No problem. It costs nothing to dream, so just pile it all on. At some level or other, everyone does it—dreams of what he or she wants in life.

Ah, but now comes the hard part—committing your entire career life to actually achieving what you say you want. As one of my business associates used to remind me, "Talk is cheap." You can sit in the comfort of your living room, reading this book, and say to yourself, your spouse, your friends, or your dog with utter sincerity that you want to run your department or the company you work for, or be made a partner in the professional firm that just hired you, or become financially independent, or spend more time with the kids.

But when you go to work on Monday, is everything you're doing with your time actually leading you in the direction of your goals? And I mean this coming Monday, not next Monday, or the Monday after you pay off those credit card loans, or the Monday after you finally leave your job and start your own company. Or are you a cog in someone else's wheel—getting a paycheck, but just doing a job that helps someone else achieve his or her goals but in reality has no clear path for achieving your own? If you are, if you're a Drifter or one of the Forlorn, and you have to change gears and become a Heat-Seeking Missile.

DON'T SELL YOURSELF SHORT

How you select your career target, what course you choose to achieve it, and how you operate from day to day to maximize the chances you'll be successful are three very different questions. The first deals with your career destination, the second with your career journey (your career path), and the third with your behavior on the journey.

The career destination you commit to most influences your chances for financial success or the impact your career will have on the world you work in. Choose to follow a path leading to becoming a CEO or superintendent of schools, and you'll earn more and have more influence than if you choose one leading to sales manager or grade-school teacher.

The journey, on the other hand, which we discuss in chapter 2, most influences how happy you'll be. Finally, in chapters 3 through 7 we'll talk about the day-to-day behavior that most influences your chances of actually achieving your goal.

So let's ignore the journey and your career behavior until the next chapters and focus now on your chosen destination, the goal you set for your career.

We have all met people whose level of aspiration seems unrealistic given their capabilities—the type of silly people who try out for *American Idol* but can't carry a tune. Interestingly, however, when it comes to the careers most people pursue, aspiring for too much is generally not the problem; it's aspiring for too little—far too little. People often fail to achieve Outstanding Success not because they are Heat-Seeking Missiles tracking a heat source they aren't capable of hitting, but because they are not shooting high enough.

Dawn was a thirty-five-year-old engagement manager with a major consulting firm. Before joining the firm, she had spent more than ten years with a federal law enforcement agency, doing work she loved but which did not lead anywhere in the agency. Which was why she left.

Although she was earning far more money with the consulting firm than she had with the government, Dawn was not happy in her job. When I asked her what her career aspirations were, her answer was to find a job that was as interesting as the one she'd held with the government. She was even willing to step backward in her career to do it.

Hold onto your hat, but finding work you enjoy is not a sufficient career aspiration if you hope to achieve Outstanding Success. It is not usually even a good strategy if your goal is to find work you'll be sure to enjoy for the rest of your career. Of course it's essential to enjoy what you do from day to day, but this should be what happens along the way to achieving a career target. It is not a career target alone.

In just wanting to do work she loved, Dawn was not shooting high enough. In point of fact, this was the strategy she'd defaulted to because she got tired of trying to find something she both loved doing and that would lead somewhere meaningful in her career. All she knew was that she wasn't happy and she had to do something to make things better, even if what she did only solved the problem for the short run.

Paradoxically, focusing only on doing what you enjoy without an eye to where it can lead can lead you to decades of working in jobs you *don't* enjoy. To take an extreme example, say you're fortunate enough to rise through the ranks in the U.S. Navy to become the captain of a nuclear submarine. You may truly love this job and want to spend the rest of your career doing it. Too bad, because after you've had your turn at this exciting command, you are for the rest of your career stationed on shore. A few of your happiest career years may be followed by years of misery.

The job you love to do may not be as exciting as submarine captain, but few organizations will give you the opportunity to do the same thing for decades and still achieve Outstanding Success. The longer you stay in the same position, the longer you block the way of younger people working their way up, which is the main reason many organizations have "up or out" policies.

But even if you hold a job like teacher, police officer, health care worker, or any of the hundreds of jobs that are ends in themselves, you're going to pay a price in earnings if you focus on only what you do and not also on where you're going. No matter how good you may be at your job, the job grading systems used by nearly all organizations will quickly stop your compensation from increasing by more than the rate of inflation. By midcareer you'll find your earnings languishing just when your financial needs may be growing.

Don't sell yourself short in deciding where you want to go in your career. You might not be capable of becoming the next American Idol or NBA MVP, but why not a CEO, university president, chief of police, school superintendent, or army general? Have the confidence to commit to a significant career goal, one worthy of all the time and energy you're going to put into your career. Then follow the advice of the rest of this book to achieve that goal.

LOCKING ON

How, exactly, do you go about choosing a career target to pursue? Some lucky people never have to wrestle with this question. The answer is obvious to them and has been obvious for most of their working lives—become the CEO of a major company, a general in the armed services, a medical researcher working to cure important diseases, a Broadway producer, a partner in a major law firm. But to most people, deciding on precisely where they want their careers to end up is a very difficult question. I have coached people in their thirties, forties, and fifties who still don't know what, not to make light of the issue, they want to be when they grow up.

I cover this topic of setting a career goal in chapter 8, "Coach Yourself," but it's useful to recognize the challenge this most basic step in career management poses for many people. First, it's important to understand the type of career goal you should *not* be setting if your objective is to be happy as well as wealthy or influential. Too often, when I ask people where they want to end up in the latter part of their career, they tell me, "I want to retire by the time I'm fifty," or "I want to be earning a million dollars a year by the time I'm forty," or "I want to be working in a job where I don't have to commute," or "I want to be able to spend more time with my children."

But these are not the kind of goals we're talking about here because you can achieve all these goals and be thoroughly miserable. The real question you want to answer is, "What do I want to be doing *at work*, and how do I want to be spending my time *at work* when I reach my career objective?" Being retired, becoming wealthy, or not commuting doesn't answer the question of what you want to do *at work*. At best, they answer the question of what you don't want to do at work or what rewards you want for working. Focus on what you want to do for forty or more hours a week, not on what you don't want to do or what you want to get paid.

Unfortunately, this makes choosing a career target even more difficult for many people, because they don't know what they want to do or where they want their career to lead them. If you're one of these people, don't fret. Eventually you will have to decide or you'll spend your entire career as a Searcher or a Drifter, a condition that will likely lead to becoming one of the Forlorn. But while selecting a career target is a critical first step in moving from a drifting career to a directed one, it is not a step you need to worry about getting exactly right the first time around. Which is a good thing, because there's a good chance you'll get it wrong the first time around. Or even the second, third, or fourth. Circumstances change, you change, life happens, and what seemed like a worthy and achievable life goal at one point may seem very different later. So it's comforting to understand that your career target need not be a lifelong thing.

John Feinstein, the prolific sports writer, tells the interesting story of Matt Cavanaugh in his book about the National Football League, *Next Man Up*. Cavanaugh played in the NFL for fourteen years before starting a second career as a coach. Feinstein quotes Cavanaugh as saying, "When I first got out of college, I thought I would end up doing something in criminal justice. That's what my degree was in. What I really wanted to do was be in the FBI. I even took some night classes my first few years in the league to prepare for applying. But as time went on, I realized that wasn't going to happen."

What happened is that Cavanaugh wound up spending far more time as a player than he ever thought possible. By the time he was through playing, it was too late to begin a career leading to the FBI. So he capitalized on his playing experience and knowledge of the game and accepted an entry-level coaching job, which he built into a coaching career.

While FBI agent to professional football player to NFL coach is not the career he envisioned for himself, it shows how someone's aspirations combine with real-life experiences to shape a career. And how wrong it's possible to be in selecting a career target and still succeed.

Cavanaugh's experience is especially interesting when contrasted with the experience of Brian Billick, the NFL head coach who figures prominently in Feinstein's book. In contrast to Cavanaugh, Billick had planned to spend a career playing in the NFL. But he wasn't good enough, and although he was drafted by the NFL out of college, he was cut and found himself out of a job early in his career. He redirected himself to coaching and became an Outstanding Success.

For one reason or another, the goal you're pursuing might lose its appeal or become impossible to attain. When this happens, you must have the courage to make changes in your work and personal life just when you're getting comfortable. To make things even tougher, these may be changes that your colleagues and family don't entirely understand or support. But a Heat-Seeking Missile is not deterred.

Which brings us from choosing your target to choosing the path you take to achieve that target. Because happiness lies not in your destination but in the journey, what you do every day in an effort to meet your career objective is as important as the career objective itself. While chapter 1 is about the destination, chapter 2 is about the journey.

OUTSTANDING SUCCESS STRATEGY #2

Stay in the Zone

In this chapter:

- What it means to work in your Outstanding Success Zone,

- Why good enough is not good enough, and

- How to find your Outstanding Success Zone.

I look on that man as happy,
who, when there is question of success,
looks into his work for a reply. . . .

RALPH WALDO EMERSON

MONEY'S FINE, BUT HOW DO YOU WANT
TO SPEND YOUR TIME?

It is popular mythology that you will be rich and happy if you do what you love. Nothing is so effective at disproving this nonsense as the undeniable fact that I would be living in a cardboard carton today if I played golf for a living.

Oh well, if you can't be successful doing what you love, maybe at least you'll be happy. Unfortunately, not even that is necessarily true.

One of my friends is a gifted woodworker whose greatest happiness in life is working in his shop. But he knows he'd end up unhappy trying to support his family on whatever he could earn building custom furniture in a one-man shop. If he expanded and built a profitable furniture business, he'd then be spending his time hiring and training people, promoting his product line, establishing distribution channels, and using automated production methods instead of the handcrafting he so loves. Instead of being a craftsman, he'd be a businessman in a highly competitive industry, trying to succeed at a business with a lot of moving parts. In other words, if he tried to earn his living doing what he loved to do, he'd wind up unhappy.

So even if you know what truly makes you happy in life, you're still stuck with one of life's most important puzzles to solve—what kind of work should you do to earn a living? Being a Heat-Seeking Missile committed to a specific career target doesn't answer this question by itself. You might decide, for example, that your career goal is to become a C-level officer (e.g., CEO, COO, CFO, CIO) in a large company. But there are hundreds, perhaps thousands of ways to achieve that goal: big companies or start-ups; consumer products or high tech; line or staff; rise through the sales ranks or manufacturing; East Coast, West Coast, or Midwest.

When we first begin our careers, we're free to pursue any goal and follow any path. As time passes we lose options. Wait long enough and many opportunities are lost completely. Maybe you can still go to medical or law school at fifty, but the odds are against you. And you're going to have a tough time at forty-five becoming a literary agent in New York City if you've spent the last twenty years auditing accounts receivable in Kansas City.

Sadly, some people never consciously decide for themselves how they are going to spend their working lives. Chance offers a first job, and time wears the tracks so deep that after a few years there's no getting out. People are in sales, accounting, law, teaching, or whatever because that's where their professional life began, and that's where they started to accumulate personal career value. After a few years, the only way they can escape is to give up much of that value and start again. So they stay for forty years where they started, rarely making a conscious career management decision after they're in their early twenties.

The path you choose to follow during your forty-year career will be the most important determinant of how happy you'll be. How do you decide? No matter where you are in your career and no matter what your personal financial goals, you decide by answering this most important question: how do I want to spend my time? Your answer sets the stage for being happy or unhappy, for reaching your career goals or not, for becoming an Outstanding Success or for just having an ordinary career. Your answer opens some options and forecloses others.

When my father was a young man he somehow concluded that being an engineer was the best, most prestigious career a man could have. Although he had quit school in the tenth grade and was supporting a small family, he went back to complete both high school and engineering school. For years he worked as an engineer, and although he was a decent engineer, he never really enjoyed his work. What he enjoyed and was exceptionally good at was selling.

But in his mind, selling wasn't a prestigious calling, and for years he bounced between engineering and selling jobs. He'd work for a while as an engineer, but not really enjoy his work and not earn a particularly good income. So he'd take a sales job, do extraordinarily well, earn big money, but soon worry he wasn't in a job people could respect. Back to engineering.

To this day I remember him describing how he finally came to terms with his career direction. One day, utterly unhappy in an engineering job, he decided to forget about what he thought others thought about his being a salesperson and do what he loved to do, what he was good at, and what would pay him what he felt he was worth. He left engineering and never returned, working first in sales and later in his own businesses, where he did all the selling. Having decided how he wanted to spend his time, he was happy and successful in his career for the rest of his working life.

With this perspective, let's look at the three ways you can choose to spend your time at work. Specifically, you can spend your time doing:

- Things you love to do

- Things you are really, really good at

- Things that will make you rich (or influential)

THINGS YOU LOVE TO DO

First, you can spend your time doing things you really enjoy doing. The circle in figure 1 represents all those things you love to do—riding your bike, playing sports, playing guitar, painting or working with wood or clay, maybe watching TV or (and?) drinking beer.

FIGURE 1

Things you love to do

Of course it's not just games and hobbies that people enjoy. There's engineering, teaching, law, driving trucks, programming, going to war, building houses. The list is endless. There is almost no work activity that somebody doesn't love to do. It may be true that they wouldn't do it if they weren't being paid to do it, but they still love it and look forward to going to work. But of course, for every line of work some people love, there are others that hate it.

Lynn and Connie graduated from public New York City colleges at the top of their class. Both worked for a period before deciding to become lawyers, and both attended the same law school, although a year apart. Lynn loved every minute of her time in law school. From her very first day she knew she'd found her place in life; she loves her work as much today as when she began decades ago.

Connie, on the other hand, hated law school from the beginning. She stuck it out and earned her law degree, but I've never known anyone so wretched and unhappy. Her remarkable will and perseverance overcame her fear of admitting a mistake and making a change she felt her friends and family would view as a failure, but this decision on how to spend her time destroyed her happiness.

You might read this story and feel you would never let what happened to Connie happen to you, and because the circumstances are so extreme, you may be right. But there's a far more insidious condition waiting to ambush your happiness: work you neither love nor hate, work that makes you neither happy nor unhappy.

To understand this better, it helps to distinguish among three possible states in life:

- Being happy

- Being unhappy

- Not being unhappy

Let's call this third state of not being unhappy being satisfied, a sort of "good enough" state of being. While the word "satisfied" might be interpreted as positive, I'm using it here in a somewhat negative sense. From the standpoint of your work and your career, it describes a condition that's entirely tolerable and perhaps even comfortable. It's good enough, but that's not as good as it could be or as good as you'd like it to be.

Being happy is a stable situation, which means it will take a significant force to cause you to change. Being unhappy, on the other hand, is an unstable situation. It takes relatively little to motivate unhappy people to accept the need for change, even if it takes them a long time to actually make the change.

Unfortunately, for most people the third state, being satisfied, is also a stable condition. It will take a significant force to cause them to change or even to realize they should change. If the money is good and you're comfortable at work, why change just because you're not entirely happy?

But for people who achieve Outstanding Success, merely being satisfied is unacceptable. Good enough is not good enough. They require more from their work—they demand that it makes them happy—and they change jobs or even entire careers when it doesn't.

At thirty-two, Mitch was already a senior executive at a Fortune 200 company, the youngest member of the board, and on track to one day become CEO. He was good at what he did, handled customers well, and had the respect and admiration of his colleagues.

But in his heart, Mitch didn't really enjoy the consumer products industry he was in, an industry he'd fallen into by happenstance early in his career. His real interest was computers, the field in which he'd earned BS and MS degrees, and he grew to feel that selling consumer products was uninteresting and unfulfilling.

Two years after being promoted to run his company's largest operating group, Mitch left the company to join a small technology consulting firm. The move meant taking a 30% salary cut and leaving a large stock option grant, but he finally loved his work again. Within five years he'd become a senior executive in the high-tech industry. Despite this success, his job change set his career progress back five years in terms of earnings and prestige, but Mitch never looked back. He was doing work that made him happy, and he worked himself back into being a top 1% earner.

THINGS YOU ARE REALLY, REALLY GOOD AT

We've established that while you should do something you love to do, this is not enough to become an Outstanding Success. Too bad, but life is just not that simple. If you want to love what you do and become an Outstanding Success doing it, you should be *really, really* good at doing it.

In figure 2, the circle on the right represents the set of all those things you are really, really good at. It overlaps, but not completely, the set of things you love to do.

FIGURE 2

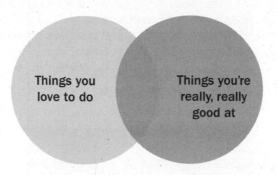

"Really, really good" means really, really good compared with others. If you carried a two handicap in golf you'd be really, really good at golf. But not compared with people who play golf for a living on the professional tour. Fortunately, unlike being able to play better than par golf, most people *can* develop the skills they need to become really, really good at things that are important in the careers most of us follow.

———————

Like Connie and Lynn, Jim also went to law school. While he didn't graduate at the top of his class, he did well and thoroughly enjoyed the intellectual experience. But he could see that a great many of his classmates were much better at the law than he was. So instead of pursuing a career in the law, he went into the securities industry, starting as an entry-level associate at half the starting salary of his law school classmates. Despite the law degree, he became a Searcher, looking for something he'd love doing and that he could be better at than others.

Jim quickly found his niche and devoted himself to studying a then-new class of fixed income securities and the markets they traded in. This was the center of his working life, and he became an undisputed expert simply because he focused all his time and energy in one area while his colleagues moved among different departments. He loved his work and rose quickly through two different financial services firms before leaving to start his own fixed income specialty firm and becoming an Outstanding Success.

The good thing for those of us who are not in a talent-based career is that we get a wide choice of things we can decide tō become really, really good at. This is because in every career there are thousands of things that need to be done well that ordinary people can learn to do really, really well if they put their minds and energy to it long enough.

With a BA degree in psychology and no business, technical, or product background, Hank received only one job offer after graduation. It was a low-paying, entry-level position in the HR department of a large bank. The bank assigned him to a largely clerical role in the employee benefits area, but he found employee benefits interesting, with its complex plans, requirements, and rules.

Happy to have any job at all, Hank decided to become an expert in employee benefits. While this doesn't take any special talent, it takes time and study to thoroughly understand the intricacies and options of employee benefit and insurance plans and their subtle effects on the companies that purchase them and on the employees they cover. Hank focused his attention and learned the details of not just the bank's plans, but alternative plans as well.

He rose quickly in the bank's HR group, always working in employee benefits, but after five years he topped out at the bank and took a job as an associate with a company that consulted in the field of employee benefits. After three years with the consulting firm, he joined an insurance company that sold employee benefits, taking a pay cut to join the company's sales force. Although he had no previous sales experience and he was anything but the typical insurance salesperson, in short order his expertise in employee benefits made him one of the company's most successful salespeople. He next used this reputation and the contacts he'd developed to start his own insurance agency, which he built into a successful business.

Whether it's employee benefits, trading securities, managing people, building systems, managing projects, or writing ads, most things done in most careers can be learned by ordinary people. But most ordinary people learn what they have to learn well enough to do whatever jobs they're doing at the moment, but not well enough so they know their areas much, much better than everyone else doing the same jobs.

Do what Jim and Hank did. Find something you love to do and become much better at doing it than almost everyone else.

THINGS THAT WILL MAKE YOU RICH (OR INFLUENTIAL)

It makes sense that you should spend your time doing only things you love to do and are really, really good at. But let's not forget that Outstanding Success also means becoming a top 1% earner or outstandingly influential in your field.

What if what you love to do and are really, really good at is writing haiku, a form of Japanese poetry written in three unrhymed lines of five, seven, and five syllables, such as:

Outstanding Success,
Without doing what you love,
Fuhgeddaboutit!

Unless you're the type of person who is going to be extraordinarily happy with extraordinarily low earnings, writing haiku poetry for a living is probably not a sound career choice no matter how good you are at it and how much you love doing it.

The lower circle in figure 3 represents the set of jobs that have you spending your time in Outstanding Success Jobs or Stepping-Stone Jobs—jobs that allow at least for the possibility of making you rich or influential.

FIGURE 3

Things you love to do

Things you're really, really good at

YOUR OSZ*

Things that allow you to achieve your goals

*YOUR OUTSTANDING SUCCESS ZONE

Of course it stands to reason that you should work only at jobs that make it possible for you to achieve your personal goals for fame, fortune, and influence, whatever they may be. But it is not always clear just what jobs these are. Unfortunately, there are a lot of jobs that, while they may provide more useful output and pay better than writing haiku poetry, offer about the same opportunity for becoming an Outstanding Success. So it is important to distinguish among five different types of jobs. They are:

- **Outstanding Success Jobs** pay compensation that puts you right up there with the 1% earners and are so much fun that you can't wait to get to the office every morning. Some of your earnings may come in the form of incentive compensation, such as performance bonuses, stock options, profit sharing, partnership shares, and not be guaranteed, but if you do your job well, it's a reasonable bet you'll average out to be a top 1% earner over time.

- **Stepping-Stone Jobs** aren't Outstanding Success Jobs, but they're steps that lead you to the Outstanding Success Jobs. At the beginning of your career, every job is a Stepping-Stone Job. Lewis Ranieri, a college dropout, began at Salomon Brothers[*] as a mail clerk and rose to become vice chairman and a major force in the financial services industry. Thomas Watson Sr., the founder of IBM, began his career as a bookkeeper and sewing machine salesman. Many people use consulting, planning, sales,

---

[*]Michael Lewis, *Liar's Poker: Rising Through the Wreckage on Wall Street* (New York: Penguin Putnam, 1989).

engineering, production, and accounting positions as Stepping-Stone Jobs. But at some point Stepping-Stone Jobs become Dead-End Jobs.

· **Dead-End Jobs** may not themselves be the end-of-the-road last jobs of a career, but they do not lead to Outstanding Success Jobs. Whether a job is a Dead-End Job depends on the job, your career objective, and where you are in your career. That Lewis Ranieri was a mail clerk and Thomas Watson Sr. sold sewing machines early in their careers did not stop them from achieving Outstanding Success. But if they were working in the mailroom or selling sewing machines at age fifty, it's safe to say they would have been working at Dead-End Jobs.

· **Gotcha Jobs** have a hold on you because they pay well *or* because you're happy doing them. ("I'd leave, but the money is too good," or "Sure I'll never be rich, but I really enjoy what I do.") But they're not Outstanding Success Jobs because they don't both pay well *and* make you happy. You should stick with a Gotcha Job if it's a Stepping-Stone but leave it if it's a Dead-End. Be especially careful not to let a Gotcha Job lull you into using up valuable career time.

· **Bad Jobs** neither pay particularly well nor make you happy. Stick it out for as long as you can if you're in a Bad Job that's a Stepping-Stone to something better, but this is the time to summon up all your courage and make a change if you're in a Bad Job that's not going to lead anywhere.

To know if you're in a Stepping-Stone Job or a Dead-End Job requires that you know where you want your career to go, and that you realistically and honestly evaluate your job in light of your goals.

As I write this, the U.S. auto industry is losing money, market share, and the hearts of car buyers worldwide. As a result, hundreds of senior executives at U.S. automakers are leaving what were once enviable Stepping-Stone Jobs. Given the state of the companies and the industry, the executives holding these jobs have determined that they were suddenly in Dead-End Jobs.

Recognizing this problem in these extreme circumstances doesn't require great insight and introspection, but in other situations, it does.

Chris is a thirty-five-year-old IT professional working as an independent contractor for a large financial services firm that has a history of ineffective IT. Frustrated with last-minute surprises about IT projects about to miss yet another deadline or budget, the firm's management hired Chris as an independent overseer to report ongoing progress on important IT systems development projects.

Chris's compensation is more than he's ever earned in the past, and his position has him working with senior managers throughout IT and in general management. But Chris is in a classic Gotcha Job—in this case a Dead-End Job without the management, budget, hiring, or delivery responsibilities he needs to move into senior IT management positions, which is Chris's goal. He's wasting time doing damage reports from the field instead of developing positive relationships with senior IT executives and accumulating the management experience and noteworthy accomplishments that will help him move into the upper reaches of IT management.

When I asked Chris where this job could lead, he had no answer, even after a week to consider the question. He was literally speechless. But instead of accepting that he was in a bad career position, he chose instead to ignore his situation. His salary, perhaps 25% more than he could earn in a Stepping-Stone Job, stopped him from making a change, even when he understood his Dead-End Job couldn't lead him where he wanted his career to take him.

———————————

To avoid Dead-End Jobs, you must continually assess your job compared with what you're trying to accomplish in your career. And while it may be difficult to do in the short term, you must not become distracted by short-term advancements, rewards, and comforts that mask a Gotcha Job that will not lead you where you want to go.

YOUR OUTSTANDING SUCCESS ZONE

Your Outstanding Success Zone (OSZ) is that relatively small intersection in figure 3 of the things you love to do; the things you do really, really well; and the things that will make you rich or influential. Stated this way, what could be a more obvious formula for achieving Outstanding Success?

But don't be misled by the simplicity of the diagram or the fundamental idea it represents. Very few people work in their OSZ. Instead, they are "satisfied" with not being unhappy with their work, with making good money, with working among congenial people, and with the accoutrements of short-term success. Or they're afraid of making changes, taking some risks, or taking a step or two backward when something moves them outside their zone.

Unfortunately, you can't become complacent even when you're working in your OSZ, because while life is grand when you're in the zone, life often conspires to move you out of it. Personal interests change, companies and industries change, or you run out of new things to learn or new things to accomplish. For whatever reason, the growth in your personal value stops or significantly slows or you just stop enjoying whatever it is you're doing. When any of this happens, it's time to move on and get back into the zone.

But most people don't. Their very success keeps them from changing. They're treated well, part of the team, given money, big offices, first-class travel, a full-time assistant. They feel important, needed, and appreciated.

I know, because I was caught in the comfort/ego trap and stayed with a company almost three years longer than I should have. I'd stopped accumulating new experiences and was repeating past accomplishments after my first three years at the job. There was nowhere else for me to go in the company, but I had been extraordinarily successful and was treated well by the firm's management, given money, a corner office, and lots of ego stroking.

All heady stuff, but none of it had anything to do with achieving my objective of moving into the highest reaches of a major company and becoming a top 1% earner. I had fallen outside my Outstanding Success Zone, but was blinded by the accoutrements of success and failed to recognize it. I've not made the same mistake again.

In summary, to become an Outstanding Success, you must work in your Outstanding Success Zone. You're in the Zone when:

• You're doing something you love to do,

• You're doing something you're really, really good at, and

• You're doing something that will make you rich or influential.

One or two of the three won't do it; you need all three. This deceptively simple idea needs a chapter and not just a single sentence because people don't understand how challenging it can be to find and stay in their Outstanding Success Zone.

But let's say you've done it—you're working in your Outstanding Success Zone. How do you make it work for you?

CHAPTER 3

OUTSTANDING SUCCESS STRATEGY #3

Maximize Your Value

In this chapter:

- Determining what you're worth,
- Staying close to the money,
- Creating a top 1% personal package,
- Experiences vs. accomplishments, and
- Your personal career value life cycle.

*Even Noah got no salary for the first six months—
partly on account of the weather and partly because
he was learning navigation.*

MARK TWAIN

DRIVEN ONLY BY MY GRANDMOTHER

You're going to spend at least forty years of your life working. That's a lot of time not riding your bike, raising your kids, climbing mountains, or doing whatever you'd be doing if you didn't have to work for a living. If you're going to give up that much of your free time anyway, why not make a lot of money while you're doing it? Specifically, if your career is in the for-profit sector, why not earn at least $40 million, the amount we've established as putting you among the top 1% earners in the country, the target for Outstanding Success? If you're in the public or nonprofit sectors the earnings potential is much lower, but why not at least be a top 1% earner in your field, even if that's not $40 million?

But why would the world pay you so much more than it pays 99% of the other people also working for a living? After all, these people presumably want to make more money just as much as you do.

There's only one reason people will pay you more: you're worth more.

In this chapter, we're going to look at how the world determines what you're worth and what you can do to increase your value. We'll start by looking at how the world determines the value of used cars. Surprisingly, the same factors that determine how much a used car is worth also determine what you're worth in your career.

Say you need to sell your car. You write an ad that puts it in the best light, not bothering to mention the dent you had fixed after you hit the lamppost while text messaging on your cell phone: "Low mileage, barely broken in, always garaged, like-new condition. Driven only by my grandmother on Sundays to and from church." This is your car's résumé, so to speak.

But now you have to decide how much to ask for the car. Three factors determine the value of used cars:

• Intrinsic value

• Supply and demand

• Unique characteristics

Intrinsic value is your car's worth independent of the other factors we'll talk about. A five-year-old Bentley is worth more than a five-year-old Buick, even if the Buick has fewer miles and the Bentley's carpeting has some Grey Poupon stains.

The second factor is the relative supply and demand for that particular model and year. If there's nothing unusual about your car, supply and demand will be the primary factors determining its worth compared with cars in the same class. Taken together, intrinsic value and supply and demand will set a value that's published by companies like Kelley Blue Book. The amount you can get for your car will vary little from what the *Blue Book* says it's worth.

Notice, however, that intrinsic value and supply and demand have little to do with your specific car. No matter how well you've maintained that old Buick, it's just never going to be worth as much as a Bentley. Bentleys are worth more intrinsically, and there are far fewer of them out there.

But the third factor determining your car's value does take into account your car's specific distinguishing characteristics. Say, for example, you're trying to sell a 1967 Corvette. This car, which originally cost about $5,000, can sell for $15,000 or, if it's in mint condition and equipped with the Chevy L88 427-cubic-inch engine, for more than $600,000.

Throw out the *Blue Book*. When a car is so unusual that its characteristics put it almost in a category by itself, prices can skyrocket. Suddenly we have a Chevrolet selling for more than a Bentley. It doesn't matter that the Bentley sold for many times more than the Corvette when they were both new.

When all three of these forces work together positively to determine your car's value—your car has high intrinsic value, it's in short supply, and it's somehow unique—you're talking about a car priced in the top 1% of used cars.

But you're not a used car. How does the world determine what you're worth? Remember, we're talking here about what you're worth in the context of your career, not as a human being. We'll call this "personal career value," fully recognizing that people worth millions in personal career value may not be worth two cents as human beings, and vice versa. As it turns out, the same factors that determine the value of your used car also determine your personal career value—the intrinsic value of what you do, supply relative to demand, and certain personal characteristics. Let's look at each in turn.

STAY CLOSE
TO THE MONEY

Not to put too fine a point on it, the objective of businesses is to make money. For the most part, the more connected your job in business is to making money, or in some cases to preventing the company from losing money, the higher will be your intrinsic value. Consequently, people in information technology are more valuable in banking than in mining, while corporate finance people in banking are more valuable than IT people in banking.

When I ran a software company, there were big differences in compensation and working conditions between the engineers who developed the software products and the salespeople who sold those products. The software engineers were all intelligent, well-educated computer scientists who were under constant pressure to develop, test, and deliver new software releases. It wasn't unusual for developers to work sixty- to eighty-hour weeks. Worse (for them), we tracked every programming error in released products back to specific engineers via a bug-tracking system, so each developer's performance problems were always on full display.

On the other side of the building we had a competent, productive sales staff. We measured their performance just as rigorously as we measured the engineers' performance, but it wasn't the end of the world if a salesperson missed her quota for a quarter or two. There was always the next quarter to make it up, as some other salesperson beat quota and saved the day. While the salespeople were all intelligent, it's unlikely their average IQ came within ten points of the engineers' average IQ, or that their average workweek was within twenty hours of the developers' workweek.

Yet the average successful salesperson earned more than twice what the average successful developer earned. Pay wasn't the only injustice the developers suffered. At the end of every year, the company treated the successful salespeople and their spouses to a four-day celebration in places like Hawaii or the Caribbean, the type of thing common in sales organizations throughout the business world.

At the end of the year, we treated the successful software developers to lunch at the local Holiday Inn, after which they all returned to the office to work on that next release.

As important as product developers (or engineers or accountants) are, salespeople are "closer to the money" and have higher earnings potential. Which is not to say you can't become a CEO and an Outstanding Success if you're a software developer, but that in most companies, *until you move closer to the money, your intrinsic value will be relatively lower no matter what job you have.*

It's the same throughout all organizations, both profit oriented and nonprofit oriented, private sector and public sector. A dimwitted CEO who spends half his time playing golf still earns more than the brilliant IT director who's at the office ninety hours a week. Investment bankers, securities analysts, and securities traders who earn huge fees for their companies earn more than engineers, accountants, and marketing people working in ordinary 8% margin companies. Incompetent school superintendents earn more than brilliantly competent teachers or principals, and lawyers working in large big-city law firms that bill clients $750 per hour earn more than lawyers who work as in-house counsels.

If your career is in business and your objective is to become a top 1% earner, it helps to select a career path that has a direct connection with helping the company achieve its fundamental objective—to make money. If your career is in the public sector or in a nonprofit, career paths leading to positions that control the biggest budgets or the most money will generally have the highest earnings potential.

As logical as this seems, people wind up twenty years into their careers working at jobs that are far from the money, wondering why their earnings aren't higher. They see how difficult their jobs are, how much experience or education they need to perform them well, and how integral they are to the ongoing operation of their organization and think, "This isn't right. I should be making more money."

But that's like thinking their outstandingly well-maintained, low-mileage, mint-condition Buick should be worth as much as the Grey Poupon carpet-stained Bentley.

DON'T BE A DIME A DOZEN

No matter how valuable your job may be to a company, the laws of supply and demand apply to you just as they do to used cars. Holding demand steady, if there are a lot of people doing what you do, your earning potential will be relatively lower than if there are few of you.

I had a keen sense of this fundamental economic force as an engineering student and as the son of an engineer. When my father was a engineer, the country depended on things mechanical and structural for growth and progress—automobiles, bridges, roads. Mechanical and civil engineers were in high demand compared with the supply graduating from the country's engineering schools, and the earnings potential in these engineering disciplines attracted the best and brightest.

By the time I entered engineering school, electronics

had become the important driver of engineering-based products, and the supply of electrical engineers couldn't keep up with demand. Not surprisingly, the starting salaries of electrical engineers became significantly higher than for other engineers. When computing became important, the demand for people trained to develop computer hardware and software exceeded supply, and the starting salaries of computer scientists led the pack. This same purely economic supply vs. demand dynamic works in all fields.

If you're just starting out, you can factor in this relative supply and demand when choosing a career, as many students do when declaring their majors. But if you're already established in a career and don't have the unlimited flexibility of a college student to choose among becoming a physician, lawyer, philosopher, or welder, you're limited to making smaller adjustments. We'll have more to say about strategies for getting unstuck from a poor position in chapter 10, but for now let's look at the more personal determinants of your career value.

BE AN L88-EQUIPPED CORVETTE

If there are many people with your experience and background, then like the ordinary used car, you will trade in a narrow range. Not unlike used car prices, these salary figures are published in surveys that show the range, from high to low, of what you're worth in various parts of the country and in different industries. You'll most probably be valued somewhere within this narrow range, and that's what you'll be paid. Moreover, you'll be paid in that range, and trapped in that range, for as long as you hold that job.

This mass pricing effect begins the day you're offered your first job. Say you start your career as a systems analyst, accountant, or consultant. Your beginning salary is pretty much the same as everyone else of your age, education, and experience. For the next five to ten years you do a good job, work hard, and meet the objectives set out for you. But that means you're doing pretty much what everyone else in your career path does. So you're right up there with the rest of the pack, the rest of the cars on the lot.

Along the way, your value increases with your experience, and your earnings increase, along with everyone else's. In five or ten, or even fifteen or twenty years, your worth will still fall into a relatively narrow (though higher) range, a range set by salary surveyors and HR departments. *As long as your earnings are determined by published salary surveys, you will never, ever become a top 1% earner.*

But let's say you distinguish yourself from the crowd, and you become the L88-equipped 1967 Corvette of technology, accounting, consulting, or toothpaste marketing. Like the unique car, your value can skyrocket.

I saw the practical result of this most dramatically one year with salaries of chief information officers (CIOs). The annual compensation packages of individual CIOs at the time ranged from a low of $50,000 to well over $3 million. The lower salaries were published in salary surveys HR departments used to set compensation. But HR didn't consult publicly available surveys to determine they needed to pay a chief information officer more than $3 million a year. Like the value of an L88-equipped 1967 Corvette, the price of the high-end IT head was determined by what the company had to pay to attract a specific candidate, however high that price happened to be.

How do you become an L88-equipped Corvette instead

of a run-of-the-mill Buick, a $3 million a year manager instead of a $50,000 a year manager? After you've chosen a career path, there are three personal characteristics that differentiate your personal career value from others with the same career path:

- Your personal packaging
- Your relevant experience
- Your outstanding accomplishments

PERSONAL PACKAGING

Every good marketer knows the importance of packaging to a product's success. BMW and Mercedes could save a bundle if they allowed their dealers to sell cars out of old warehouses down by the docks and if they printed their brochures on ordinary copy paper held together by a staple in the corner. But luxury car dealerships are as pristine and staged as luxury model homes, and their brochures look like costly coffee-table books.

Pringles potato chips don't come in those cylindrical packages because the company down the street that makes tennis balls bought too many tennis ball cans and gave Procter & Gamble a good deal on the overstock. Pringles packaging is more important to the product's success than is the product's taste.

Apple's iPods weren't named iPods instead of Ipods because the capital *I* on Steve Jobs's printer wasn't working. It was part of a carefully thought-out product package.

While none of these packaging characteristics changes

the product itself, they influence its attractiveness to the target market and, consequently, its perceived value. Your personal packaging similarly affects your value.

You may never have thought of yourself as having packaging, but you do. Your personal packaging is the sum total of your appearance, personality, speech, manners, sense of humor, intelligence, confidence, dress, smile, and mannerisms. Some of this you can manage and some you cannot, but don't despair if you come up short in a few areas. There's still a lot you can do to manage your personal packaging, and the things you can manage will usually more than compensate for the things you can't. Specifically, you control your grooming and how you dress, your manners, whether you look people in the eye when you talk to them, whether you listen carefully and respectfully before you talk, your knowledge of and interest in the world around you—politics, sports, the arts, business—and if you're in good physical condition or a couch potato.

The passion you show for your work is also a large part of your personal packaging.

I was once looking to hire a head of marketing for a company I was running. The candidate we were scheduled to interview showed up ten minutes late and was more than a hundred pounds overweight. His clothes looked as if they'd come straight out of the laundry bag, and his hair was dyed two different colors—rust and purple—which I have never seen on hair before or since. My immediate thought upon seeing the candidate was, "Our recruiter has lost his mind."

But we found that the candidate was passionate about high-tech marketing, and especially about measuring the results of every marketing dollar he spent. He loved the creativity and challenge involved in designing and running marketing campaigns and measured to two decimal places the number of new prospects and dollars of sales he was able to generate per marketing dollar he spent. He showed us charts and graphs of the results of his past efforts the way proud grandparents show grandchildren's photos to anyone standing still. He talked of past campaigns he'd run with the enthusiasm of a child and the pride of an Olympic gold medalist.

Here was a person truly passionate about his work, and we hired him instead of other candidates with far more conventional personal packaging. (Interestingly, when he showed up for his first day at work, his hair was a standard-issue single color.) His performance over the next several years never disappointed us, and the sales staff loved him.

Whether you're early or late in your career, if you care about achieving Outstanding Success, you should think through your personal packaging carefully to understand how people see you in the context of what you're trying to achieve. And don't talk to me about all this being superficial and shallow. Of course it is, but these personal characteristics influence the value people place on you in career settings. You ignore them at your peril, even if you try to pretend you're above such nonsense. Successful people don't ignore these issues, whatever their personal feeling may be about their relevance to what's important in life. They know personal packaging affects their perceived value, and they act accordingly.

RELEVANT EXPERIENCE

Fortunately for those of us with bad hair, personal packaging is only one of three personal factors that go into the formula for determining our career value. The second factor is the *relevant* experience we've accumulated. The key word here is "relevant."

Say you've just accepted your first job in the accounting profession as part of an accounting firm's audit group. You work for the same company for six years, first doing heads-down accounting, then as a supervisor, then as a team manager, and finally as an account manager. You're constantly learning, continually adding new experiences to your résumé. But if your objective is to become the chief financial officer of a large company in the odd-shaped plastic object industry, is this experience really moving you toward achieving Outstanding Success?

In the beginning of your career, it's reasonable to assume that your experience will be useful in preparing you for the CFO position, particularly if you've been assigned to work with clients in your chosen industry. But before long, your experience begins to become less relevant to your CFO goal and more relevant to success in an accounting firm, which is not your objective. From the standpoint of eventually becoming a large-company CFO, you may have wasted the last three or four of your six years at the accounting firm. Maybe you've made good money, learned a lot of stuff, and had your ego stroked, but too bad; when it comes to moving toward becoming a large-company CFO, others have passed you by.

This disconnect between experience and personal value occurs regularly in all organizational functions, including IT, sales, accounting, finance, project management, engineering, and production. People get tricked into accumulating *irrelevant* experiences because companies hire and promote to fulfill *their* needs, not yours. You get raises and promotions, and it feels so good you never see what's happening to you until it's too late.

You need to think like Robert, whose career goal was to move out of his technical specialty and into general management.

I was the CEO of a high-tech company when I hired Robert to run a failing technology group that was critical to my company's success. Through technical competence, sound management practices, and good leadership, he turned his area around in nine months. Spectacular performance, and everyone recognized it as such.

But as soon as he'd done the most important job I'd hired him to do, he came to me and said he wanted to run a sales region. He had no experience in sales, he had barely gotten things settled down in his technology post, and I resisted. But he was relentless, cornering me at every opportunity, telling me he could do for the company in sales the same thing he did in his technology group. He was an outstanding performer, and CEOs don't ignore outstanding performers, so I eventually gave in and put him in charge of a struggling sales region.

Robert went at this new responsibility with the same zeal he'd brought to his first assignment, and after a year his performance was good and improving, if not outstanding. Nevertheless, he felt he'd learned all he had to learn in the position, and he asked that I put him in charge of all marketing and sales. This time I refused and held firm. He was clearly a rising star, but I felt he needed more experience in sales before I could trust him with marketing and sales for the entire company.

Despite his success at my company, dramatically rising compensation, and fast-track career, within six months he left to run marketing and sales for another technology company. Less than two years after that, his new company made him chief operating officer, and eighteen months later he left that company to become CEO of a third company. In six years he managed his experience so he could go from being unqualified to be a CEO to actually becoming the CEO of a medium-size public company. Although he was successful in the jobs he held along the way, he never lost sight of his goal, which was not just to succeed in his jobs, but to gain the experience he needed to become CEO.

ACCUMULATE OUTSTANDING ACCOMPLISHMENTS

By far the most important component of your personal career value is not your experience, but what you've accomplished while you've gained that experience. To understand the enormous difference between experience and accomplishments, compare the following:

Doing Things	Accomplishing Things
I attended college.	I graduated at the top of my class.
I studied languages as a minor in college.	I speak fluent French, Arabic, and Farsi.
I was a product manager.	I conceived of and introduced the most successful product in the company's history.
I ran the chicken feed division.	I turned a division that hadn't made a profit in five years into a top performer in twelve months.

While personal packaging and experience are important at the beginning of your career, *it is outstanding accomplishments that quickly become the currency of Outstanding Success.* This is the standard stuff any good résumé writing coach will tell you, but its importance to Outstanding Success transcends your résumé, which is, after all, just an after-the-fact record of what you've done.

Accumulating significant accomplishments requires a finely tuned awareness of how you spend every working day. To achieve Outstanding Success, it is not enough to spend your time just doing things, even if those things are the essence of your job. To become a top 1% earner, you must dramatically increase your personal career value by single-mindedly and relentlessly focusing on delivering outstanding accomplishments. Outstanding accomplishments are your L88 engine, the thing that so greatly increases your value that your career value skyrockets. The next chapter, "Swing for the Bleachers," talks about this at length.

Geoff's first job after leaving college was product manger with an unprofitable start-up company. He managed a staff of one—himself. His job was to design computing products that encouraged customers to subscribe to and pay for computing services his company provided.

By itself, this job would have provided good experience and added to Geoff's career value. But unlike the company's other product managers, Geoff took a different path.

The company's model for product development was that it invested in developing products and then recovered their development cost from customers paying to use them. Too often, however, the products failed to generate enough customer interest even to cover their cost, much less provide an ongoing profit.

Reasoning that a start-up needed to save every dollar possible and reduce the risk that products wouldn't pay back their development costs, Geoff decided a better approach would be to persuade a customer to pay for the development of his product up front. This was not part of his job description, and he first had to persuade the regional salespeople to take him along on calls so he could meet and form relationships with customers. He was soon spending two full days each week on the road, meeting with prospects and customers.

This continued exposure allowed Geoff to understand specific customer needs in great detail. When he proposed a solution to a senior manager at a key prospect, the manager agreed to fund the product if his firm could influence its specifications. Because the customer paid all the product's development costs, the product was profitable on the day it was launched. This was a first in the company's short history, and it set the gold standard for future product development efforts. And because a customer worked closely in its design, the product met a real market need and its sales grew to account for 20% of the company's revenue.

This was a significant accomplishment for someone in his first job and added greatly to Geoff's personal career value. Which was fortunate for Geoff, because the company, going through the trials and troubles many start-ups experience, eventually had to reduce staff by 50%. Not only was Geoff the only product manager to keep his job, he was the only employee who was promoted and given a raise at the same time the company was downsized.

YOUR PERSONAL CAREER VALUE
LIFE CYCLE

Let's end this discussion of personal career value by looking at personal packaging, experience, and accomplishments from the perspective of your personal career value
life cycle.

Your total personal career value will follow a predictable pattern throughout your career. In the beginning,
people bet on your potential, which they judge based on
weak and, frankly, unreliable evidence. This will include,
for example, where you went to school, your appearance,
and whatever little experience and accomplishments you
have accumulated.

During the early part of your career, experience will,
for a while, contribute to increasing your career value.
Before long, if you are destined to achieve Outstanding
Success, accomplishments will become far more important. It is not that all three—personal packaging, experience, and accomplishments—don't always contribute to
your career value, but their relative importance changes
dramatically for those who achieve Outstanding Success.

So if you're just starting out in your career and you have
an Ivy League degree and a Harvard Business School MBA,
don't get complacent. Your education and early achieve-
ments will initially open doors that may be closed to others.
In the long run, however, it is significant career accomplishment that makes the difference. And if you're a state
school graduate whose college career was closer to *Animal
House* than you ever want your parents to know, don't fret.

Say two people begin their career the same year. One
has an unimpressive physical presence and a 2.2 GPA

from a no-name state college, but has achieved outstanding accomplishments during the early part of her career. The second looks good in a suit, graduated from an Ivy League school with a 3.5 GPA, has a Stanford MBA, and has gained several years' experience but hasn't chalked up accomplishments. It isn't long before the state school graduate leaves the Ivy Leaguer in the dust.

In summary, the weight of your personal value will move from personal packaging, to experience, to accomplishments as you move through your career. It is only with the addition of significant accomplishments that you will be able to break out of the HR department's salary increase guidelines and become an outstanding earner and eventually an Outstanding Success.

It's not enough just to have your personal career value increase over time. Most people's personal career value increases as they gain experience. To achieve Outstanding Success, your personal career value has to increase so it's greater than 99% of the people you work with. Fortunately, we have the formula for doing this:

- To the extent possible, work at jobs close to the money.

- Put together a "personal package" that is consistent with being a 1% earner.

- Develop a high-value skill that puts you in high demand.

- **Accumulate outstanding accomplishments while you accumulate experience.**

The last of these four is in boldface type because it is by far the most effective and fastest way to maximize your value. How exactly you accumulate outstanding accomplishments is the subject of the next chapter.

CHAPTER 4

OUTSTANDING
SUCCESS STRATEGY #4

Swing for the Bleachers

In this chapter:

- Earning $40 million,

- Escaping the gravitational pull of the HR department,

- The meaning of Outstanding Performance,

- How to manage your boss,

- When to run away, and

- The Outstanding Performance question.

You'll never get ahead just by being really good at what you already do. Top management will look at you and say, "Hmmm, okay, just keep doing it."

MICHELLE PELUSO, AGE 34
CEO, TRAVELOCITY

JUST HOW HARD IS IT TO EARN $40 MILLION?

We know that Outstanding Success is being happy with your work and having career earnings in the top 1%. It is a concept that applies to the long term, to a career. To get to Outstanding Success we need another concept— Outstanding Performance.

Outstanding Performance is a concept that applies to the short term, to what you're doing right now. Outstanding Performance is performance so unexpected in the context of a particular job, and so valuable to your organization, that it is noted and applauded by people above your boss. It is performance that makes you, the people who work for you, your boss, and maybe even your boss's boss, into stars in the eyes of people who matter in the organization. It is the organizational equivalent of a home run, and invariably, it is performance that is not even contemplated as part of your job description.

To understand where Outstanding Performance fits into your career life, we need to look at the forces that affect your pay and understand just how hard it is to earn $40 million over the course of a forty-year career and be among the top 1% earners. Is this such a big deal, or is it something anyone can do who works hard and performs well in every job along the way? So let's go behind the scenes to look at what's behind your pay raises.

Let's say you're just graduating from college and beginning your career in your first professional job. Assume your starting salary is $50,000 a year and inflation averages 3.5% during your career. If your earnings increase at the rate of inflation, your forty-year career earnings would total $4.2 million, a long way from $40 million.

But you're full of energy and ambition, raring to attack your career and do a great job in every assignment, so of course you expect your raises will far exceed the rate of inflation. And for a while they do, because young people begin work with so little experience that their personal career value increases rapidly as they gain experience. At the same time, the salaries of older workers who are no longer advancing in their careers level off, and retiring, highly paid workers are replaced with younger, lower-paid workers. The net effect is that wage increase dollars flow from older workers to younger workers, making it possible for younger workers to receive increases greater than the rate of inflation even though the workforce as a whole receives wage increases that barely match inflation.

So let's allow for larger increases in earnings in the early years, an assumption that's supported by a U.S. Bureau of Labor Statistics report that shows the average real wages increases in the second column of the table below.

Ages	Average Real Wage Increases	Wage Increases Assuming 3.5% Annual Inflation
22–25	6.5	10.0
26–30	4.0	7.5
31–35	3.6	7.1
36–40	2.5	6.0

Because the second column shows the increase in your real earning power (after inflation eats into how much your actual raise will buy), we need to increase these raises to account for inflation. Assuming a constant 3.5% rate of inflation, you could expect, on average, to receive the increases shown in the third column of the table.

On the face of it, the increases in the third column seem pretty impressive for the under-forty crowd. Ten percent, 7.5%—not too shabby, especially when you consider that the national average wage increases for all workers have just barely kept pace with inflation. But what this means is that average wage increases for workers forty-one and older are considerably below the rate of inflation (3.5% assumed here). But let's be wildly optimistic and continue to increase your salary at 6% from age forty-one to retirement. Even with these optimistic assumptions, your total lifetime earnings will be $10 million. Not bad but still far below the top 1% earner level.

So even if you start out at $50,000, you never have a bad year, and your compensation grows nonstop for forty years at far above the national average, a $40 million career is nowhere in sight. For the average person, even this is wildly optimistic. You need a better plan.

Before discussing how to break out and become a top 1% earner, let's understand one of the most powerful forces working to keep your salary increases low—the human resources department's compensation system.

THE HR TRAP

Despite the tough-guy image many managers—both men and women—like to project, when it comes to controlling salary costs, most managers are wienies. I know I am, and it's simple to understand why.

Say you're a manager with a bunch of people reporting to you, people on whom you depend to help you achieve your own career objectives. All other things being equal, you want these people to like you and go the extra mile for you when the time comes. Of course people will love and follow you if you treat them well, provide them enjoyable work, and show your appreciation. But how much money you pay people still has a lot to do with how happy they're going to be working for you.

Managers know this, so there's a natural tendency for them to want to give the people who work for them big raises: "Ten percent, twenty percent—sure, why not? You've worked hard, I know you and Blanche need the money, and we're going to have to put in some long hours on the Fritzblat project coming up this next quarter." You know very well that if you give out 2% to 3% raises for a couple of years, you'll be in the office until midnight, dealing with Fritzblat on your own.

Which is precisely when, and why, the managers run into the human resources department and its highly structured and limiting compensation system. While these systems vary somewhat among different organizations, they are all remarkably similar.

Jobs are assigned grades, and job grades are assigned salary ranges based on objective salary surveys done by compensation consultants. No matter how well you've done or how much your boss likes you, the job grading system makes it almost impossible to earn more than the maximum of your job grade range. But there's an even more limiting force at play that works to limit salary increases even for people who are far beneath the maximum of their job grade.

Each year, every manager typically receives a salary increase pool equal to a certain percentage of the total pay of the people reporting to her. Say your boss is allowed to give out salary increases totaling 5%. This means that if she gives you a 15% increase, she has to give someone else much less than 5%. Even though managers might want to give some of their top performers big increases, and even if the job grading systems allows them to do so, they really, really don't want to tell other people who work for them that they're receiving significantly less than average. Consequently, salary increases tend to bunch around the average, in this example, 5%.

This wouldn't be a problem for you if salary increases regularly averaged 10% to 15%. But they don't. Organization-wide increases of 2% to 6% are typical, even within successful, rapidly growing organizations. These HR systems are rigid and regimented and guaranteed to limit the raises you'll receive over the course of your career.

You may now believe I feel these HR-driven compensation systems are bad things. You would be wrong.

Without these systems there would be chaos and economic disaster as salary costs spiraled out of control. I believe in these systems, have helped to create them, and support them wholeheartedly. I just don't want them to apply to me. Or to you if you're looking to achieve Outstanding Success.

These HR compensation systems are fair, effective, and necessary, but if you expect to become an Outstanding Success, you must escape their gravitational pull. And the way to do that is not just by doing your job, but by delivering Outstanding Performance.

OUTSTANDING PERFORMANCE

We said that Outstanding Performance is performance so unexpected in the context of a particular job, and so valuable to the company, that it is noted and applauded by people above your boss. Outstanding Performance is what you have to do to accumulate the accomplishments we talked about in chapter 3 that so dramatically increase your personal career value. Outstanding Performance separates you from the rest of the organization and takes you out of the controlling tentacles of the HR department's compensation system, which limits the compensation growth of ordinary employees. It opens the door to the compensation mechanisms reserved for only the top levels of an organization. These include substantial stock option grants, performance shares, discretionary and formula-driven annual bonus awards, deferred compensation, and a wide variety of schemes devised by organizations to help them retain their outstanding performers.

One year after Eliot was hired as plant manager, he received an 8% salary increase and options on three thousand shares of company stock to add to the five thousand shares he was awarded when he was hired. This was pushing the limits of the HR department's compensation system, but even if he continued at this rate, he would never have become a top 1% earner. But his performance was so outstanding that after eighteen months the company promoted him over a dozen more senior candidates to head the company's most important operating unit. His salary doubled, he received an additional option grant of fifty thousand shares, and his bonus at the end of the second year tripled.

For the next several years, Eliot's base salary remained unchanged, but his bonuses, set by the compensation committee of the board and not the HR department, continued to increase at double-digit rates as a reward for delivering Outstanding Performance. The value of his stock option awards increased even more rapidly.

It's not necessary to be CEO or another senior officer

to deliver Outstanding Performance. During the summer between Eliot's freshman and sophomore college years, a small manufacturer of precision electric motors used in military aircraft hired him to help out in the plant. Helping out meant doing every dirty or tedious job in the plant no one else wanted to do. If it was possible to have a lower level job in the company, no one had yet thought of it. For many people, this could have been the setting for a miserable summer. But not for Eliot.

He'd do the jobs he was assigned with equanimity, then look for more interesting and useful work to do. As he became familiar with the plant's operation, he noticed motors stacked up each day in a rework area. He'd bring the motors to the people in quality control to learn why they failed to pass the company's rigid quality tests. Then he had the hourly people in production teach him how to use the different machines in the plant so he could rework the motors and get them back into the production line.

Before Eliot became involved, rework was a costly disruption that interfered with the plant's ongoing flow. After one month into his summer job, Eliot was single-handedly keeping the rework area clear of the previous day's quality control rejects. Along the way, he'd become familiar with all the company's products and learned every aspect of production. He did so well, the company's management put him in charge of the plant for the two weeks the plant manager went on vacation.

At the end of the summer, the owner offered to increase Eliot's salary 50% and pay for the rest of Eliot's college education if he would work for the company full time and attend school part time. It was the first time this small company had ever offered to subsidize an employee's education.

Eliot was grateful but refused because he wanted to finish college in four years. But the point is that it's possible to deliver Outstanding Performance in even the most entry-level job. Eliot's performance was far beyond his boss's and the plant owner's expectations, and it directly contributed to making the business successful. If working for this company had been consistent with Eliot's career goal, he would have been on his way to becoming one of its senior executives, and he was only nineteen years old at the time. So no more excuses for not becoming an outstanding performer because you're not high enough up in the organization.

MANAGING YOUR BOSS

Do the job you've been assigned to do, the one described in your job description and the one with the HR department's job grade attached to it, and you'll be trapped in your organization's compensation system forever. To escape, you have to deliver Outstanding Performance— performance beyond what anyone would ordinarily expect from someone in your job.

Fine, but who determines what you have to do to deliver Outstanding Performance?

Don't expect the definition of Outstanding Performance to be in your job description or for someone, even your boss, to come along to tell you what it is. Your boss may be incompetent or lack vision; or she may have her own agenda, maybe just planning on gaining experience and moving on to a new job; or she may be doing something she thinks is important but that in fact is not at all important to the organization.

If you expect your boss to set your objectives, you will never deliver Outstanding Performance or achieve Outstanding Success yourself. But even if your boss is competent and has the company's best interest at heart, *you almost always have to set your own objectives if you hope to deliver Outstanding Performance.*

This may at first sound like corporate anarchy, but setting your own objectives is a good thing for you, for your boss, and for the organization you work for. To start, whether you have an entry-level or C-level job, whether you're in line or staff, it forces you to understand the organization's purpose, objectives, and strategies and how you fit in and can influence them.

If you think this is no big deal, that surely everyone already knows their organization's goals, you're wrong. In *The 8th Habit,* Stephen Covey refers to a study of twenty-three thousand people working in business organizations. Nearly two-thirds did not know their organization's goals. Not one of these people had a chance of achieving Outstanding Success.

When Roy was hired to head up a company's large information technology (IT) function, it was not at all clear what he could do to deliver Outstanding Performance. The company's corporate management wanted IT costs lowered, and that, along with continuing to provide reliable, effective service, formed the basis of Roy's job description.

But after studying the company's financial statements, talking to senior operating mangers about the company's business plans and strategies, and meeting with vendors and IT colleagues in the industry, Roy concluded that it wouldn't be possible to reduce IT expenses and still support the business as the operating managers needed it to be supported. His job description and objectives were a recipe for failure, something he would not have known before it was too late had he not been searching for a way to deliver Outstanding Performance.

Looking for a source of funding that would allow him to continue to grow IT services without using more of the company's own resources, Roy proposed that the company commercialize some of its IT capabilities and offer them for sale. The initial efforts were successful enough that the company made a series of supporting technology acquisitions that became a separate profit-based operating division under Roy's leadership. Roy was a success within the company and went on to become an Outstanding Success in his career. But to do it, he had to set his own objectives and not allow himself to get lost in his job description.

———————————

Managing your boss is an unusual concept for most people, who are conditioned to think that their boss's job is to manage them. But that's not really the case at all.

Your boss's job is to achieve a set of objectives that somehow relate to what the organization is trying to accomplish. As part of this arrangement, your boss is assigned resources to help her out, and you're one of these resources. Managing you is a derivative duty, like having to prepare a budget every year, or maybe planning the annual holiday party—something that has to be done but that doesn't contribute directly to meeting the organization's objectives.

If you view managing people or leadership as an end in itself, it's understandable how you may believe that managing your boss or leading from below could cause conflicts. It's as if you're usurping her hard-won responsibilities. But if you view managing people and leadership as means to an end and not as ends in themselves, it's no big deal if your boss doesn't have to manage or lead you. In fact, it's a relief. Whenever someone with competence and vision who works for me takes the reins and manages me—leads me from below—the outcome is always better than if I'm forced to provide all the management and leadership myself.

The idea of managing your boss and leading from below may seems like a radical, self-centered, and potentially dangerous approach to career management to people accustomed to thinking of organizations as rigid hierarchies. In practice, it's a straightforward three-step process that's embraced by everyone involved because everyone comes out a winner. The process is:

1. Understand your organization's important objectives, plans, and strategies. You may have to get out of your office and into the plant or meet with customers and others in the company, and you may have to do this on your own time, but you'll never have trouble finding people eager to talk with someone truly interested in the organization.

2. Set your objectives so they demonstrably contribute in some way to achieving the organization's important objectives.

3. Set your objectives so they will help your boss become an Outstanding Success.

The best thing about this approach is that it's honest. When you line up your personal objectives with those required to make your boss and your organization successful, you're doing what's best for everyone, and you can be aboveboard at all times.

WHEN TO RUN AWAY

If you want to achieve Outstanding Success, you need to be a home run hitter. Not every time up at bat necessarily, but with reasonable consistency. You can't do this without swinging for the bleachers, which means working at jobs that make it possible for you to deliver Outstanding Performance.

Unfortunately, without being aware of it, many people work at jobs where it isn't possible for them, no matter what they do, to deliver Outstanding Performance. Sure, they can do an excellent job and receive top performance ratings year after year, and they can earn the biggest raises the company can give in whatever job they're supposed to be doing. But they're locked into HR's compensation systems, and they cannot achieve Outstanding Success.

Tony, a thirty-five-year-old IT specialist, landed what he thought was a dream assignment with a large telecommunications company. Because he was an expert in his field, the company hired him at a premium rate to be on site and available whenever a question arose in his area of expertise. Paid for forty-five hours a week, he estimated he worked no more than three hours a day. While the job was a low-stress assignment that paid outstandingly well, and everyone he worked with loved and supported him, the job offered no possibility to deliver Outstanding Performance. Tony was on a fast track to becoming one of the Forlorn.

At one time I believed it should be possible to find a way to deliver Outstanding Performance in any job, but I now know there are times when that isn't true. Specifically:

- **The unimportant line or staff function**. You work for a staff function that supports the organization, but that in no way can contribute meaningfully in helping the organization achieve its primary purpose. Staff functions such as IT, legal, accounting, human resources, transportation, and security can be critical to the success of some companies, while in others their role is inconsequential and routine, and they receive little senior management interest or attention. Or you may be part of a line operation that isn't important to the organization's strategy, perhaps a business that will be sold or closed when the time is right.

   While there are no line or staff functions from which it isn't possible to become an Outstanding Success, there are functions in some organizations from which it isn't possible. They're just too far away from what's important to the organization.

- **The personal agenda boss**. Your boss or managers above your boss may have a personal agenda that isn't consistent with delivering Outstanding Performance, a distressingly common phenomenon. For example, if your boss is a few years from retirement and interested only in maintaining the status quo until he can escape to a condo in Florida, or if the company's management is emotionally committed to a product line that new technology has made obsolete, there may be little you can do to deliver Outstanding Performance in your job.

- **You're odd man or woman out.** For some reason,

the people who matter don't really like you. It happens. You didn't go to the right school, or you went to the right school and they didn't. Your approach to life or work is different, or you come from the city or the country and they come from the country or the city. You drive a Mercedes and they drive five-year-old Buicks, or their kids go to private schools and yours attend PS 105.

There are hundreds of reasons why you might not fit in, and if you don't, little you do will be embraced. In these situations, the people who matter won't judge your performance impartially. Even more important, you won't be given the freedom and support you need to deliver Outstanding Performance. If you don't fit in after trying the best you can, don't fight it.

· **The failing company.** The company you work for is failing, and there's nothing anyone can do about it. Perhaps the industry is dying or the competition dominates or the product is moribund. Often great successes come from turning around troubled companies, but not every business can be saved. In the public sector, not every cause is worthy of your efforts and support. When there is truly nothing that can be done and the ship is destined to go down or just doomed to flounder forever, it's time to abandon ship.

If your goal in your career is to achieve Outstanding Success, you should never agree to work at a job in which it's not possible to deliver Outstanding Performance.

Never. It doesn't matter how good the money is, how much you enjoy your coworkers, how short the commute, or how good the benefits. Run away.

THE OUTSTANDING
PERFORMANCE QUESTION

The best way to avoid being in a position where it's impossible to deliver Outstanding Performance is to do your homework before you accept a job. Ask your interviewers the Outstanding Performance Question, which is: "If I take this job, what is it I can do that my boss and his boss would consider to be absolutely Outstanding Performance? I'm not just talking about doing a good job, but doing a job that is so good and contributes so meaningfully to the organization's success that everyone would consider it to be absolutely Outstanding Performance."

Then sit back and wait for an answer. Be quiet; it may be hard but don't say anything. Let the person you're talking to think her answer over carefully.

Don't accept an answer that's just a description of fulfilling the job's responsibilities. For example, for a sales position, making your sales quota isn't Outstanding Performance. It's your job. But if you get an answer like, "Ya know, if you could turn around the Dallas region, which has been a disaster for us since the competition moved in, that would be outstanding," or "If you could get the competition's biggest account to drop the competitor and use our products, that would be outstanding," then you're on the right track.

Be wary of organizations where no one in the management group you'll be reporting to can answer this question or if the answer is essentially, "We'll just be happy if you do your job well." Sure, they'll be happy, but you'll never become an Outstanding Success.

Interestingly, taking job interviews in this direction will help you land the job if it's the right job for you. Suddenly the people who are interviewing you will understand that you're not just interested in a job, you're interested in a job where you can deliver outstanding results that directly help everyone in the company. It puts you in a different class.

If you already have a job, you should ask yourself (or your boss) the Outstanding Performance question periodically—perhaps as often as once a quarter. What can I do in this job that would be considered Outstanding Performance? Just be careful to answer in the context of the organization's needs and not just as part of your job description.

Hal ran a large data center supporting a Fortune 200 company. The data center operated with a service reliability of 99.0%, beating the unit's goal of 98.5%. Hal reported to me at the time, and I asked him the Outstanding Performance question during our annual planning session. After careful thought, he told me that improving reliability to 99.5% would be Outstanding Performance. He was wrong. He confused doing things that were hard to do with things that were important to do.

While moving from 99.0% to 99.5% would have been very difficult, no one would have noticed or cared. The sad fact was that the data center's users disliked the data center despite its already high reliability. So instead of focusing on the technical measures of data center performance, we identified all the reasons for the users' dissatisfaction. As it turned out, user unhappiness centered on the data center management's responsiveness to user requests and not on technology or performance issues. This perspective changed everything.

Instead of focusing on hard, costly technical and service problems, of which there were few, we resolved instead to concentrate on the softer, human interactions causing user enmity. With considerable trepidation, Hal committed to shift his group's attention from improving statistically measurable performance to raising user satisfaction to the highest levels.

Making people happy is a very difficult assignment, especially when they start out hating you, as was the case in this situation. It took three years, but Hal succeeded in turning around user satisfaction so dramatically that an independent consulting study rated the data center as one of the top two such operations in the country. Hal's reputation grew, and he moved from data center management into seven-figure chief information officer positions in several large, prestigious companies.

No matter how careful you are, you can still wind up in a job where Outstanding Performance isn't possible. If that happens, don't stew or complain, don't rationalize, and don't accept a hand that's turned bad. I've left jobs that turned out to be different from what I thought— one after a single week and one after four months that required a cross-country move. When you or your circumstances change, it's important to accept reality and embrace whatever changes you need to make to put you in a job where you can deliver Outstanding Performance. You have to be in a position where you can swing for the bleachers. It's the only road to achieving Outstanding Success.

Okay, so there you are, locked onto a career target like a Heat-Seeking Missile, working in your Outstanding Success Zone, and doing a job where it's possible to deliver Outstanding Performance. Perfect, except that now you have to do it. Which brings us to perhaps the most important strategy for achieving Outstanding Success—doing what you say you're going to do. You've got to deliver the goods.

CHAPTER 5

OUTSTANDING SUCCESS STRATEGY #5

Deliver the Goods

In this chapter:

- Keeping promises,

- Focusing on what matters,

- Setting high levels of expectation,

- Measuring individual performance,

- Hiring for strength,

- Not betting on superstars, and

- Preventing failure.

Undertake not what you cannot perform,
but be careful to keep your promise.

GEORGE WASHINGTON, TAKEN FROM
Rules of Civility & Decent Behavior in Company and Conversation

KEEPING PROMISES

People learn early in life that they should keep their promises, and they grow up believing that promises are sacred. That is, until they begin their careers. For some reason, people who would feel terrible if they failed to buy a promised toy for their children, not show up as promised to help move a friend to a new apartment, or visit the in-laws as promised are remarkably unaffected by their failure to deliver on promises made at the office.

Salespeople say they're going to make their sales quotas, but in software sales, for example, the statistics tell us that each year 40% fall short. IT people commit to delivering systems on time and within budget but almost never do. It is hardly unusual for senior executives to miss revenue and earnings targets.

You would think all this failure to do what they say they're going to do would teach people to stop promising more than they can deliver. But no failure to deliver on a promise at the office seems embarrassing or egregious enough to stop people from just making more promises they fail to deliver on.

Leading, planning, motivating, managing, talking the talk, and all the other organizational folderol that takes up your time at work doesn't count for anything if you don't execute and consistently do what you say you're going to do. *To become an Outstanding Success, you must consistently deliver the goods.*

Of the seven strategies for achieving Outstanding Success, Deliver the Goods is the single most important, especially since what you say you're going to do is deliver Outstanding Performance. It is also the most difficult strategy to put into practice—it's where the real work of achieving Outstanding Success begins. Unfortunately, there is no easy secret to turn you into someone who can consistently deliver Outstanding Performance, but there are six operating principles that will take you a long way. They are:

• Focus on what matters.

• Set high levels of expectation.

• Measure individual performance.

• Hire for strength.

• Don't bet on superstars.

• Prevent failure.

While up to this point we have focused entirely on how you should manage your career, we now turn to how you should manage your resources—specifically, your time and the people and money the organization assigns to you. The result is a change to the tone and focus of the book for the rest of the chapter—from personal strategies to more nuts and bolts management. But it's a change we can't avoid. To tell you to go out and execute well without providing guidance on exactly how to execute well would be like telling you to go out and make a lot of money if you want to be rich. Your response might well be, "Uh, thanks, but exactly how do I do that?"

The six Deliver the Goods principles are operationally oriented rather than career management oriented. But they are an integral part of achieving Outstanding Success.

FOCUS ON WHAT MATTERS

Try the following experiment. For two weeks keep track of how you spend every minute of your day from the time you get up in the morning to the time you go to bed. To make it easy, divide your time into only three categories—those things you're doing that directly contribute to delivering Outstanding Performance; those things that are important to you outside of your work life, such as spending time with your family or exercising; and everything else. But remember, just because you're at work or doing work that's part of your job description doesn't mean you're working toward Outstanding Performance.

I have done this myself for months at a time, and what I found profoundly changed the way I worked and managed my personal time and the time of the people reporting to me.

If you're like me, and like most people, you'll find that distressingly little of what you do at work contributes to delivering Outstanding Performance.

Every hour, every day, every week, and every month, you're pulled in dozens of different directions with a to-do list that grows endlessly—projects you're a part of, meetings to attend, travel, reports to do, training, administrivia. You're always busy, always working hard, but you're being sucked into the organizational black hole that makes time disappear. The end of the month, quarter, or year rolls around and you've done a lot of stuff, but you haven't delivered Outstanding Performance. No one is standing up and shouting, "That was amazing—absolutely outstanding." If that's the case, you're doing your job, but you're not heading toward Outstanding Success.

If you're a young employee, perhaps your only resource is your personal time. If you're a manager, your resources include not just your time, but the time of the people you have working with you and the money and resources the company's budget has allocated to you. But whatever your position, the simple problem is that you have limited resources available to do all the things on your to-do list, and most of what's on your to-do list has little to do with delivering Outstanding Performance.

It's a sad fact, but organizations are like internal combustion engines—terribly inefficient systems that get a shockingly small amount of useful work out of the energy that goes into them. Like internal combustion engines, organizations lose 80% of the energy in their fuel to heat, friction, and incomplete combustion.

If you want to succeed, the secret is not to work harder or more efficiently, but to get rid of most of what's on your to-do list. Don't waste your energy and your resources producing useless organizational heat or overcoming friction. Don't become more efficient at doing the wrong things. You must instead focus all your resources on those activities, and only those activities, that will produce Outstanding Performance. It's as simple as that.

Well, that's not entirely true. There is one other type of activity you should devote some of your time and resources to—activities that allow you to avoid an Outstanding Failure.

An Outstanding Failure is an event that, if it happens, will destroy your chances of achieving Outstanding Success. If your job is to bring in an important project on time and within budget, spending two hours a week doing that pesky weekly status report and filling out time sheets may not get you closer to delivering Outstanding Performance. But if you don't do it, you get fired. So "wasting" time doing the report and filling out the time sheets prevents an Outstanding Failure.

Ed ran his company's largest data center during a period of rapid technological change. He focused his team's attention on keeping the data center on the cutting edge of technology during a tumultuous period when departmental servers, relational databases, and personal computers were overtaking centralized computing.

He was a hard worker, technically brilliant, and a good leader who was able to keep his operation relevant and effective in a changing world. But when users asked for simple, straightforward changes they needed to support their operations, such as an update to old software their business depended on, Ed's group was too busy with things they considered more important to respond quickly.

Bad decision. Failing to keep the data center's users happy was an Outstanding Failure Possibility, and in less than a year after the corporate IT head hired Ed, the users revolted. They caused him to be fired despite the advances he'd made in his operations.

Outstanding Failure Possibilities are at all levels of the organization. When I was a CEO, it would have been easy to consider the time I spent preparing for meetings with my board of directors and the meetings themselves to be a waste of time. One good customer call or meeting with employees was more important to the business than any ten board of director meetings. But if you're the CEO and you lose the board's support, you lose your job—definitely an Outstanding Failure Possibility. So I prepared very thoroughly indeed for the board meetings.

The most important rule for achieving Outstanding Success is to focus all your resources on delivering Outstanding Performance while devoting only enough resources to all other activities to avoid an Outstanding Failure.

Sounds logical and easy, but in practice it is not easy at all. Let's consider the annual budget. There are always more things to spend money on in organizations than there is money available to spend. Engineering projects, research projects, IT systems, product improvements, regions to expand, people to hire, facilities to build or repair, businesses to fund, training to provide. The list is endless.

Each of these projects has a sponsor, a living, breathing person who believes in the project and whose life is affected if it's not funded. So allocating resources is not an impersonal thing—it is an intensely people thing. As a result, there's a tendency for managers to spread the available resources among the different projects and their sponsors so as to be in some sense fair. The unspoken objective is to make as many people happy as possible while still meeting the organization's needs.

Emotions and interpersonal relationships have as much—and often far more—influence on how organizations allocate resources as does the merit of what the resources are being allocated for. In the end, good resources go out the organizational tailpipe or are turned into useless organizational heat.

When it comes to deciding how you're going to use your time and resources, you must fight this normal human predilection to be fair and evenhanded like the plague on

Outstanding Performance that it is. First, identify your Outstanding Failure Possibilities. Plan to spend whatever time and money you need to prevent these disasters, or you're toast. But after these few do-or-die resources users, the rest of your time and resources should go only to projects and activities that will lead to Outstanding Performance. And this applies not just to how you allocate your budget, but also to how you spend every hour of every day you're at work.

Barry worked in sales at a large, successful durable goods company. The company's senior management quickly identified Barry as a high-potential employee. The human resources department placed him with a similar group of future stars they planned to groom for top management positions, giving the company a large pool of people from which they hoped would emerge the managers of the future. As part of this program, the company rotated the high-potentials through different jobs throughout the company for assignments lasting six months to three years. One of the most coveted assignments was to be an executive assistant to the company's CEO.

The company offered Barry many different management development assignments, including that of executive assistant to the CEO. But he turned down nearly every one, including the assistant to the CEO position, because he did not feel these jobs would give him the opportunity to deliver Outstanding Performance. Instead, he asked for difficult sales assignments that no one else wanted, such as managing problem customers, converting large customers from competitive products, and turning around the federal sales division, which had underperformed for years.

He succeeded in all his assignments and rose far faster in the company than colleagues who spent their time becoming "well-rounded." Outstanding Performance trumped outstanding experience.

SET HIGH LEVELS OF EXPECTATION

Expectations—what you expect of others—are funny things. If you expect little of people, that's what they'll deliver— little. But expect too much, and guess what, you'll still get little. You even get little if you set the right level of expectation but the people you're working with don't see value in meeting your expectations or don't see a realistic path to achieving them. To consistently deliver Outstanding Performance, you must do the following:

- Expect a lot of people, but not so much that what you expect is impossible for them to achieve.

- Help people understand what's in it for them to meet your level of expectation.

- Show people, or otherwise make them believe, they can find a realistic path to meeting the expectations you've set.

- Establish a culture and mind-set where excuses for not meeting expectations are not acceptable.

If you do all this, people will rise to meet your level of expectation, not because you expect more of them or because they see you as an inspirational leader, but because they expect more of themselves. Which, in the end, is what will make you an inspirational leader.

When a Fortune 100 company hired Frank to head up the company's IT function, the department's eight-hundred-person systems group had not delivered a single system either on time or within budget for the past five years under three different IT leaders. The department's record was so poor for so long, and so representative of the performance standards in IT throughout industry generally, that the company's management just assumed promised systems would never be delivered on time and within budget. Worse, the department's managers and systems developers assumed the same thing.

Frank, on the other hand, came from a manufacturing background where everyone expected everyone else to do what they said they were going to do. Meeting budget and schedule commitments was the ordinary course of events, something taken for granted. Not meeting your commitments was unacceptable. So Frank refused to accept IT's poor performance as inevitable and resolved that under his leadership all systems, 100%, would be delivered on time and within budget.

Now, if this objective was truly impossible to achieve, setting this level of expectation would have done nothing to improve the department's ability to deliver on its promises. It may even have served to lower the department's already low morale. But Frank knew that it was the department that set the budgets and time schedules it was failing to meet, and that the department controlled all aspects of systems development projects. So he was able to make a compelling case to the department's systems developers that they should be capable of fulfilling promises they themselves made and were fully in control of delivering on.

Working with the department's managers, Frank instituted new procedures for setting realistic project budgets and schedules and for managing projects. He set the goal of delivering on the department's promises as the group's primary focus. In the beginning, he played an active role in helping systems managers set project budgets and schedules, and he refused to be pressured into making promises just to keep users happy, a habit the department had gotten into as a way to delay user discontent.

During his first year as IT head, Frank also participated in every project management review meeting, which he insisted be held weekly for every project, and refused to accept any excuses for project slippages once a manager had committed to a budget and schedule. He made it a matter of pride that in a field where failure to perform was the accepted standard, all the department's projects would be delivered on time and within budget. He made it a matter of embarrassment and disappointment if a project was even a day late.

The result was that for the six years Frank ran the department, nearly every system was delivered on time and within budget. The results so improved the department's standing within the company that the annual fights over project funding stopped. As soon as the company's IT users understood they would get whatever they were willing to pay for, they were willing to pay for much more. Frank and the entire IT department prospered.

Contrast these results with those of Will, who took over the sales function for a struggling technology company. Will was a high-energy, can-do manager brimming with enthusiasm and optimism. He set out to increase his company's sales in one year from less than $5 million annually to more than $20 million.

His first act was to increase the sales quotas of his salespeople by 100%. An articulate speaker and likeable manager, he gave motivational talks about being winners and moving the company to greatness. But the experienced salespeople knew the sales problem was a product line that had fallen seriously behind that of a large and competent competitor. The result was that every good salesperson left the company, even those who had been with it for years and were patiently hoping for the company to find its bearing and again assume its role as a product leader. Will set an unrealistically high level of expectation and then failed to show a realistic path to meet it.

Frank did what Will did not. He set expectations that were extraordinarily challenging but achievable. He worked through a concrete implementation program to achieve the high level of expectation he'd set. Will, on the other hand, just set stretch objectives and hoped people would be so motivated they'd rise to the occasion and somehow figure out how to achieve them. Finally, Frank stayed on top of progress from day to day and reacted to every small success and shortcoming, while Will left the details to others. Frank was a leader—Will played at being a leader.

MEASURE INDIVIDUAL PERFORMANCE

Imagine yourself in the following situation. You're asked to pull against a rope as hard as you can. First it's just you alone pulling on the rope, and you know a strain gauge at the other end of the rope is measuring how hard you're pulling.

Next you become part of a team of three other people, all pulling together on the same rope as hard as they can. Again, the strain gauge measures the group's effort. The question is, will you pull harder as part of a team or when you're pulling alone, or will there be no significant difference?

Given the effect of team spirit and that with a team you're pulling in front of other people, it seems logical to guess that you'd probably pull harder as part of a team. But it doesn't work this way at all.

Researchers tricked the subject of the experiment into believing he was pulling with the group, but in fact, he was pulling alone both when he was pulling alone and when he thought he was pulling with the group. The results were startling. This and other studies showed that people reduced their individual effort by 18 to 66% when they acted as part of a team compared to when they acted alone! Yet they believed their efforts were unchanged.

These results are famous in social psychology and have been replicated for many different tasks, including shouting, clapping, pumping air or water, cycling, editing, evaluating poems or editorials, typing, detecting signals, and even brainstorming for new ideas. Moreover, as the size of the team increases, the amount that people loaf increases.

Social psychologists call this phenomenon social loafing, and it even exists on a national scale. Private farm plots in Soviet Russia occupied 1% of the farm land, but produced 27% of the farm output. In Communist Hungary, private plots occupied 13% of the farmland and produced 33% of the country's farm output.

Okay, so there you are with your team, and your challenge is to deliver Outstanding Performance. Before you would have given your team a pep talk and had them go out and win one for the Gipper. But now you see a group of people who aren't likely to pull their own weight, no matter how great a team you may think you've assembled. What do you do?

All you have to do to eliminate social loafing is figure out everyone's role in delivering Outstanding Performance, see to it that everyone has measurable short-term deliverables consistent with his or her role, measure every person's *individual* performance against these deliverables, and reward people based on their objectively measured performance.

This is actually a lot of time-consuming, detail-oriented, nuts-and-bolts management stuff, and so perhaps it's not surprising how infrequently this is done regularly in organizations. It takes a leader willing to devote the time and energy every year or even every quarter to start with group goals and work downward toward short-term, objectively measurable deliverables for each and every person reporting to her. But if you're a manager and you don't do it, you will have a tough time consistently delivering Outstanding Performance.

HIRE FOR STRENGTH

Do a good job at work, and before you know it, you land in a position where you get to choose the people who work for you. That's when the real fun begins.

Oversimplifying somewhat, you've got three hiring strategies:

- Hire to avoid failure.
- Hire for balance.
- Hire for strength.

Hire to avoid failure. No one ever says he hires mainly to reduce risk and ensure survival, but in reality it's what many people do. It's the strategy of choice in most organizations, because not delivering Outstanding Performance has far less negative consequence than does outright failure. But if you hire to avoid failure, you're almost guaranteed not to achieve Outstanding Success.

Hire for balance. What could make more sense than to hire people who are, or who seem to be, well-balanced? These are people who, in the opinion of the hiring manager and the HR department, have good potential, will fit into the company culture, are qualified to do the jobs for which they're being hired, and who do not have glaring weaknesses, especially weaknesses that would cause turmoil or discord in the organization. As it turns out, if your objective is to deliver Outstanding Performance, there can be plenty wrong with this strategy.

Hire for strength. Achieving Outstanding Success requires people who can consistently deliver Outstanding Performance, people who can set extraordinarily high goals for themselves and deliver month after month, quarter after quarter, and year after year. Such people typically have one or two outstanding strengths, but often one or two outstanding, sometimes even scary, weaknesses.

People who hire and promote for strength focus on a person's strengths and protect the organization from the strong person's weaknesses. The protection part takes energy and creative organizational design, and at best still results in turmoil as the other people adjust for somewhat deviant organizational behavior. But as long as the person's behavioral peculiarities or weaknesses don't involve discriminatory, abusive, or illegal behavior, the result is almost always a higher-performing, though admittedly less elegantly functioning, organization.

Earl, a twenty-five-year-old who was running his own small handyman company selling its services to households, applied to my company to be a salesperson selling multimillion-dollar software products to sophisticated businesses. He had no training in technology or sales and had never worked for anyone but himself. He had certainly never sold multimillion-dollar products or even sold to or worked with businesses before. There was almost no end to the list of his weaknesses relative to the position we needed to fill.

But we also saw several strengths. He seemed very smart, motivated, and articulate, and he was responsible for generating all the business he and his partner did in the handyman business. He was soft-spoken but self-assured, the kind of salesperson we felt would do well with our prospect base and our sales engineers. He was also an entrepreneur.

We decided to hire him but protect him and the company from his inexperience by starting him in positions where he could learn without doing damage. He quickly rose through the ranks and within two years became the company's best salesperson. We bet on his strengths, worked around his weaknesses, and wound up with someone who could help deliver Outstanding Performance.

DON'T BET ON SUPERSTARS

You've got a big job ahead of you. You've set high expectations for your group, and you're determined to execute and deliver Outstanding Performance. So of course the first thing you want to do is go out and hire only the best people.

Wrong! Maybe you'll be lucky and find the best people, but on average you'll find average people. You may pound your management chest and claim to be able to attract top-quality people, but you, like the rest of the world, will be governed by the laws of statistics. Which means that while you're sure to hire an occasional superstar, the people you hire will reflect the population you're hiring from. So like it or not, the likelihood is that the people you hire will be, plus or minus a little, pretty average. To believe otherwise is to be in denial.

But wait, what about the country's top law firms, investment banks, and consulting firms, which hire only the top graduates from the top colleges? Surely the people they hire are better than average.

Well, yes and no. Certainly the people these firms hire are in some way better than people drawn from the general population of college graduates—maybe smarter, harder working, more creative. But these firms are paying a premium to hire from a different population—the population of the top 5% of college graduates. Even this subgroup has its own distribution and its own average. Among the top law school graduates, for example, there is a distribution of capabilities, and only a small percentage will become stars in the demanding environment of big-time law. Most of the others will be about average for their cohort and never make partner.

That's how the laws of statistics work. Every group has its own average and its own distribution around that average. For some groups the average is higher than for others, but the people you hire from that group are going to be distributed around that average. Nature set it up that way, and if you think you're going to hire only above-average people, it's you against Mother Nature. My money's on Mother Nature.

So one reason not to depend on hiring only the best people for whatever job you have before you is that, realistically, you're not going to be able to do it. But an even more important reason not to depend on hiring the superstars is that if it turns out they are not in fact the superstars you thought they'd be, you won't find that out until they've failed to deliver.

What is the best hiring strategy? Simple. Of course, try to hire the best people you can possibly hire. But don't obsess about it.

Gordon was a young executive for whom everything had gone well. He earned an undergraduate degree with honors from an Ivy League university and an MBA from the Harvard Business School. After his MBA, he worked for one of the country's most influential consulting firms and rose quickly, based on his intelligence and personality. He so impressed one of his clients, the CEO of a Fortune 200 company, that the CEO hired him to run a billion-dollar in sales business, despite his youth and lack of previous management experience. Gordon was smart, attractive, articulate, a hard worker, and lucky— a combination most of us can't rely on to become successful.

Unfortunately, he also believed that the key to success was to hire only people who were proven performers and who were equally smart, attractive, articulate, and hardworking. He lasted less than eighteen months in his job. The business he was managing was growing rapidly and needed its management team to grow with it. Yet Gordon was so obsessed with hiring only the very best people that key jobs remained unfilled for the entire

time he ran the division. He lost his job, in part because
he failed to staff key functions on a timely basis. Insist-
ing on hiring superstars, he failed to hire people who
could do the jobs that needed to be done.

Plan your work with the assumption that in the end
you'll be hiring average people from whatever group
you're hiring from—some better, some worse, and a whole
lot hovering around the average. This means you should
structure jobs so that you can deliver Outstanding Performance with a realistic mix of people—a few superstars,
a few losers who get by your best efforts to avoid losers, but
mostly average people.

As a simple example, let's say you're a CEO or head of
sales, and Outstanding Performance this year is to sell $10
million of your company's products. The mistake many
managers make is to look for "killer salespeople," people
who can far outsell their peers. Bad plan.

True killer salespeople are difficult to find and attract,
and they often fail to perform well when they change companies. So instead of hiring five salespeople who you believe can bring in $2 million each, hire twelve who can
bring in $1 million. Build their sales plan on a $1.2 million quota, train them well, support them, monitor their
performance, and provide coaching throughout the sales
process.

One or two will be stars, maybe bringing in $1.5 to $2.5
million. One or two will fall far short no matter how much
you help them. The rest will, on average, do $800,000 to
$1.2 million, and you'll have done what you said you were
going to do without having to rely on the ability to identify
and hire only superstars.

Each year you'll nurture the few superstars you were lucky enough to find and move your losers out in an effort to make your total staff better than average. Good for you. But then a superstar or two will leave for greener pastures, and you unwittingly hire one or two more underperformers along with some more average salespeople. So even if you've been at it for a while, you should not allow yourself to get to the point where your success depends on superstars.

In manufacturing, it is often said that a great manufacturing plant is a boring plant. There's not much excitement, and nothing much goes wrong. It succeeds by doing the same ordinary things repeatedly. It doesn't need a cast of superstars or Herculean efforts to succeed. Whether your job is to bring in sales, deliver systems, service customers, develop products, keep the books, or move the goods, it is up to you to structure and staff your operation so it functions like a great manufacturing plant—you succeed when ordinary people do ordinary things in a predictable, ordinary way.

PREVENT FAILURE

A favorite management aphorism is that a manager's job is to pick good people and then get out of their way. If there was ever a principle that made managers seem like true captains of industry, this is surely it. It assigns the job of actually doing things to the little people while raising the manager's job—picking good people—to a far higher level. Too bad, but rather than being a formula for success, this management maxim is a recipe for almost certain failure.

The problem is that it presumes you are able to consistently hire good people and that the people you hire are able to figure out how to succeed. Statistics and the real world say you're likely to lose on both accounts.

Now, don't take it personally, get all defensive, or try to tell me this is my problem and not yours. The facts are that more than four out of ten new hires fail in their jobs within three years! Indeed, in real life a good manager is not an ace at hiring good people, but someone who knows he's going to make a lot of mistakes and acts accordingly. With a 40% failure rate, or even a 20% or 10% failure rate if you're a certified hiring ace (which you're not), you're still going to hire a bunch of people who fail.

But it's worse than this because even good people fail from time to time. Maybe they don't understand their new organization's culture, or they're in a new job with unfamiliar requirements, or they have management weaknesses or blind spots, or they don't know when to ask for help, or they have distracting problems in their personal lives, or dozens of other things that can cause good people not to succeed.

So then what? The manager who believes that "My job is to hire good people and get out of their way" has a ready answer. Fire the laggards! Maybe that makes the manager feel like a macho manager and provides a ready excuse to hide behind (the other guy did it), but listen closely. Ultimately, all that matters is that you've failed, you're not going to deliver Outstanding Performance, and you're not going to become an Outstanding Success. No matter how good an excuse you have and no matter how many people you fire, failure is failure.

But worst of all, you've allowed some good people who work for you to fail. Shame on you.

The right management philosophy is summarized by

an informal contract you should make with your boss and with your people. That is, "If my people succeed, they get the credit. If my people fail, it's my fault."

So of course one of your jobs is to hire the best people you can and give them the support and resources they need to succeed. But as important, you must work with them as closely as needed to help them not to fail. With some people this may mean delegating and getting out of their way. But for others it may mean day-to-day micromanagement. The amount you should be involved depends on the amount you need to be involved for any particular individual to succeed.

This simple approach to management life becomes your guide for when and how much to delegate and how to balance autonomy and micromanagement. Above all, it forces you to never lose touch with the details of whatever you're responsible for.

If you focus your resources on what matters, set high levels of expectation, measure individual performance, hire for strength, structure jobs so average people can deliver Outstanding Performance, and prevent failure, you will dramatically improve your chances of consistently doing what you say you're going to do. This is true even if what you say you're going to do is deliver Outstanding Performance.

People who consistently deliver Outstanding Performance are in such short supply that being a member of this elite class is the single most important step you can take to becoming an Outstanding Success. The final two strategies discussed in the next two chapters, acting as if you own the business and not self-destructing, are easy in comparison.

CHAPTER 6

OUTSTANDING SUCCESS STRATEGY #6

Take Ownership

In this chapter:

- Why you should act as if you own the organization even if you don't, and

- Why selfish employees are good for organizations.

The two qualities which chiefly inspire regard and affection are that a thing is your own and that it is your only one.

ARISTOTLE

YOU DID WHAT?!

My parents were entrepreneurs. They started at the bottom, and through an unlikely collection of disparate small, sometimes struggling businesses, worked their way to the middle. With no income other than what they could earn from their businesses, my parents made every business decision as if their future and their livelihoods depended on it, which of course they did. With no funding other than their personal investments, they spent company money as if it were their own, which of course it was. They hired people as if they personally had to pay their salaries, which they had to.

Like most self-made entrepreneurs, their guide to how to manage and run a business didn't come from the *Harvard Business Review,* an MBA, or any formal business training. It came from an uncommon common sense. They were never confused about how to make business decisions, how to treat employees or customers, or how to act—they acted as if they personally owned 100% of the stock of the business because they did own 100% of the stock of the business.

I grew up never giving any of this a second thought. Then I entered the business world, a world where I was surrounded not by people who owned the business, but by people who worked for the business. It was a world where everyone was using Other People's Money.

It was as if I had entered a country populated by too many people unfamiliar with the country's customs, people who did not have a frame of reference for making decisions or acting. Examples abound of deviant organizational behavior so common that most people don't even recognize how dysfunctional it is.

- Department managers measure their stature and success based on the number of people working for them and the size of their expense budget.

- IT people and engineers make technology decisions for their organization based on the technologies they're interested in working on and what experience they want to show on their résumé instead of what's best for their organization.

- Salespeople and company lawyers negotiate with customers as if the purpose of the negotiation were to beat the new customer into submission and win bragging currency that can be spent at the next off-site meeting.

- Unless restricted by company policy, employees traveling at company expense rent luxury cars, stay at expensive hotels, and eat meals so costly they wouldn't consider paying the same amount for a meal if it were their fiftieth wedding anniversary.

- Managers make purchasing and hiring decisions with little regard for the cost to the company and without thoroughly researching the alternatives.

As counterproductive as these behaviors are, the big trouble comes when people make bad decisions that have long-term consequences.

Managers who don't instinctively treat the organization as if it were their own prepare annual plans and budgets that are disconnected from the organization's strategy and direction. For example, a division manager in a company I worked for budgeted for increased staff and a major upgrade to his business's manufacturing system when he knew the company's plan was to sell the division. Sadly, this manager's boss, also someone who didn't act as if he owned the business, approved the budget because he didn't want to hurt his relationship with the division manager—someone he'd worked with for years. When the CEO learned of the investment, his outraged response was simply, "You did what?!"

Far worse has been an epidemic of mergers and acquisitions that are fun and exciting to do and make all the managers involved feel like masters of the universe, but that make no business sense whatsoever. Studies show that two-thirds to three-fourths of M&A deals fail to increase the value of the companies doing the deals. This finding is consistent across a wide variety of industries and over many years. Yet managers continue to do stupid deals that objective, competent businesspeople using common sense would see as having "loser" written all over them.

Indeed, investment bankers who collect astronomical fees for advising clients on M&A deals are often secretly contemptuous of their clients' intelligence and business sense. They manipulate managers' egos to encourage them to do deals that generate large fees for the advisers but add no value for the shareholders.

And finally, there are managers who believe the key to career success is organizational politics, people who approach their careers much the way many actual gov-

ernment politicians approach theirs. Instead of spending their time and energy delivering on promises that
demonstrably contribute to their organization's success,
their attention is on developing internal political alli-
ances, behind-the-scenes manipulation, subtly denigrat-
ing the perceived competence and character of internal
competitors, and winning the support of those in the
power positions. Their motto might be, "Who you know is
more important than what you do."

I watched both the best and worst of this behavior at a
large Fortune 100 manufacturing company. One of the
manufacturing divisions needed to upgrade its production planning and control systems. The division controller,
to whom IT reported, favored building the system using
just the division's internal IT resources, a decision that
would greatly expand his responsibilities and increase
his importance within the division. The division manager,
knowing little about IT, supported this decision because
the controller, a classic corporate politician, had lobbied
behind the scenes to gain wide-based support for his
plan.

The head of IT, on the other hand, an experienced
systems developer, knew this was a poor decision, sure
to exceed budget and schedule and likely to do the business great harm. He favored buying a system from a
commercial vendor, a decision that he knew would be far
less risky and would not require large staff increases.
His counterproposal actually lessened his potential importance in the company because he would be managing
far fewer people if the new system were purchased from
a vendor rather than built internally. He was convinced,
however, that this was the right business decision for
the division, the decision he would make if he owned the

business. But to prevail, he had to defy the controller, to whom he reported; the division manager (his boss's boss); and the supporting department managers who would be using the new system.

In the end, the IT manager won out but only after a gruesome internal political battle. But the incident served as an extreme example of a manager who acted in the company's best interests battling against one who put his own needs first.

TAKING OWNERSHIP

Thinking of the many senior executives who have become infamous because they treated the treasuries of the public companies they ran like their personal checking accounts, I was at first hesitant to title this chapter "Take Ownership." So let's just say that this title doesn't mean that if you're the CEO it's okay to fly your dog cross-country in the corporate jet, host your spouse's birthday party in Europe at company expense, or gold plate the faucets in your company-paid Park Avenue apartment. You shouldn't do these things even if these are the things you might do if you actually owned the company.

If you're just an ordinary employee perhaps hoping one day to be the CEO, you shouldn't rent Jaguars on business trips, order the $120 wine with a business dinner that includes just you and other company employees, requisition a $1,600 ego desk chair for your office, or charge the new couch for your apartment on your company credit card because you happen to be a little short this month. (I have seen all of this done.)

Perhaps a more appropriate title for this chapter would

be "Take Ownership and Act as If You're So Sensible with Your Money That You'd Still Drive a Ten-Year-Old Toyota Corolla No Matter How Much Money You Made." While this may be a terrible title for a chapter, it's a perfect description for the way you should make decisions and for how you should spend your organization's money. And it doesn't matter whether you're the receptionist or the CEO, whether you're working for a small company or one of the Fortune 100, or whether you're in the private or public sector.

Note that this doesn't say you have to be so sensible you'd personally drive a ten-year-old Toyota Corolla in your actual life. When you travel on vacation, for example, you may use your own money to rent sports cars or Hummers, but when you travel on business, you should rent the smallest, least expensive car that will fit however many people you have to carry. And you should expect that everyone who works for you will do the same.

On the other hand, being sensible doesn't necessarily mean being a tightwad. Extremes in spending—either too much or too little—are rarely productive.

One of my friends knows a CEO who required that ten employees share every PC. Sure, he saved money on computers, but he lost more in productivity and morale than he gained in lower computer costs.

What we're talking about here is a balance based on the true needs of the organization, not on your personal preferences, habits, or desires. This balance doesn't apply just to how you spend the company's money. It extends to all decisions you make—including the risks to which you expose your organization, and to the people you choose to hire, fire, or not fire.

You may read this and feel that I'm preaching that it's every employee's moral duty to look out for the best interest of whatever organization you happen to work for. If you're in the private sector, for example, the conventional wisdom is that it's your moral obligation to work to maximize shareholder wealth. That's not the message here at all. I'm telling you to take ownership, to act as if you own the organization, for very selfish reasons—because it's necessary for you to achieve Outstanding Success.

To be successful you will have to depend on many people in the organization, people both above and below you in the management hierarchy. You will have to marshal resources others are vying for, get people to follow you, win approval for your proposals from your bosses, get the freedom to set your objectives, and ask people to make personal sacrifices. If you fail occasionally, you must survive to fight another day without losing too much support or credibility.

You cannot accomplish any of this over an extended period if people believe you're out for yourself, if they believe you're not always acting in the organization's best interests. The fact is, acting in the company's best interests always works in your own best long-term interests, because it will result in people trusting and supporting you. It is an essential approach to your career if you hope to achieve Outstanding Success.

More than that, taking ownership provides a personal North Star for guiding your behavior at work that simplifies decision making. When facing a complex decision, you no longer have to weigh the effects different options have on you, your boss, or anyone else inside or outside the organization. All you have to ask is, what is the best decision for the organization? Granted, this is not always an easy question to answer; sometimes it may take courage to make the right decision in the face of political pressure, and sometimes you may get it wrong. But in the end, this approach will keep you and your career headed in the right direction.

Taking ownership is an operating principle that applies to every person in the organization. Al has been my physician for many years. When he was sixteen years old he took a part-time job working for a restaurant owned by Marriott. Fresh at his first day of work after a previous job at McDonald's, he found himself working for a young, untrained supervisor who was unprepared for his new employee. Distracted with other issues, the supervisor told Al simply to keep himself busy. Al looked around and asked himself, "What would I do if I owned this place? How can I make this a better place to visit?

One thing that had bothered Al at McDonald's was that customers put their chewing gum under the tables before eating their meals and left it there. Over time, it became as disgusting as it sounds, even to a sixteen-year-old boy. Assuming it was the same at the new restaurant, Al took a scraper and began the terrible job of scraping chewing gum into a large cup.

While he was under a table doing this, he looked out at two wingtip shoes and a pair of dress pants standing in front of the table. Peering out, Al politely asked if he could help the man, who in turn asked what Al was doing. Al explained that people routinely left their gum under the tables, and since Al had just started and had some free time, he'd decided to clean the table bottoms because he didn't think gum under the tables was either sanitary or good for business.

The man got down on his hands and knees and looked under that tables, which certainly surprised Al, who by this time guessed that perhaps the man worked for the chain as someone who went around doing surprise inspections. Al asked if this was the case, and the man confirmed that he did work for the company and part of his job was to visit the company's restaurants. Then the man went to a phone, and Al could hear him talking to people at the home office, telling them that a sixteen-year-old had identified an important problem in the company restaurants that needed immediate attention. It turned out the man Al talked to was Bill Marriott.

Bill Marriott was so impressed with Al's ability to identify with the company that he spent time talking with him and learning about his plans for the future. Although Al planned a different career entirely from one in the food service industry, Mr. Marriott nevertheless suggested that if things ever changed and Al wanted to work in his industry, he call Mr. Marriott personally at any time in the future.

The point of this story is not just Al's instinct to treat the company as if he owned it, but also Bill Marriott's instinct to do the same thing, even though the Marriott organization was a publicly traded company and the Marriotts were not sole owners. Here we had two people, one at the very bottom of the company and one at the very top, worrying about chewing gum under the tables because both, despite their different positions, treated the company as if they owned it.

THE SELFISH EMPLOYEE

Until this sixth strategy, we've had career strategies that put you first: pick a career target and stick to it; do what *you* love to do, what *you're* good at, and what will allow *you* to achieve *your* career objectives; maximize *your* personal career value; set *your* own objectives at work no matter what your job description may say, and don't work at any job that doesn't allow *you* to deliver Outstanding Performance; focus your resources on what *you* need to do to deliver Outstanding Performance and achieve Outstanding Success.

This is all centered on you and not the organization you work for. Moreover, common to all this advice is the need to change and move on if your job isn't consistent with these strategies. Even taking ownership is something you do because it ensures you continue to get the support you need from the people around you—it's good for your career.

But what about all those people you work with who are so important to your success, people you've become friendly with, maybe even see socially? Shouldn't you consider the effect your career decisions will have on them?

And what about the organization you work for that has promoted you and given you all those raises and new opportunities? Don't you owe the company your loyalty for taking a chance on you, perhaps when others wouldn't, or for how well it's treated you over the years? If you really acted as if you owned the company, wouldn't you make personal sacrifices for its good and the good of the people who work for it? Wouldn't you put others' needs above your own?

These questions about loyalty and personal sacrifice are important because people periodically have to make career decisions that trade off career selfishness against the needs of the organization they work for and the people they work with. Do you leave for a better opportunity or stay with the company that gave you your first break? Do you leave the people you've hired to come work for you, people who had good jobs at other organizations and who have come to depend on you, or do you stick it out and sacrifice your own career opportunities?

People need a framework to think through these commonly occurring decisions. It's a framework built upon three basic beliefs that explain why it's easy to follow the book's career-biased strategies and still act as if you own the organization. From the standpoint first of a for-profit business, a company whose purpose is to make money for its owners, the beliefs are:

- You have a responsibility to provide value for your pay.

- Organizations are not human.

- People act in their own self-interest.

You have a responsibility to provide value for your pay. This is the simple idea that we all have a responsibility to do what we're paid to do and to do it as well as we can. This is a fundamental pillar of business that encapsulates what it is employees owe the organizations they work for. Without this strong sense of responsibility, the business world collapses. Indeed, all organizations collapse.

Organizations are not human. This is simply the nonjudgmental, self-evident observation that the company whose name is on your checks, whether it is a corporation, partnership, or sole proprietorship, is nothing more or less than an abstract legal concept. It has no feelings and no needs. It cannot make decisions nor treat you well or poorly. It cannot owe you loyalty and you cannot owe it loyalty, because these concepts are meaningless to something that is nothing more than a legal paper with a fancy corporate seal that now rests in a dusty file cabinet in a lawyer's office.

You may respond that your feelings are for the people who work for the company, not for the company per se. So while it may be true that you owe the company nothing, perhaps you owe the people who make up the company something. But the third belief lifts this burden of guilt.

People act in their own self-interest. Psychologists know that people act in ways that fulfill their personal needs, even when they are fulfilling the needs of others. This is not a bad thing. People give to charity because doing so fulfills some personal need. They sacrifice their own lives for their children's because even this fulfills their personal need to protect their offspring and send their genes into future generations.

What this all means in terms of your job is that if you've received raises, promotions, and opportunities over the years, it was because giving you these raises, promotions, and opportunities somehow fulfilled the personal needs of the people who gave them to you. What you received were not gifts or charity—they were a fair exchange for value you provided to the company and to the people with whom you work. One way or another, you earned whatever you were given.

Of course, if you were too young and inexperienced to yet provide your company compensating value, a case might be made that people were investing in you based on the expectation of a future return, and that in this case you owe something to the people who invested in you. But if these same people invested in a stock and it didn't pay out, would they make the same argument that the stock owed them something? No. In point of fact, the investment was made for the expectation of future return, and it is the nature of investments that they don't always pay out as expected.

Unless you have an explicit agreement about what you are to do in return for whatever investment is being made in you (and such an agreement need not be in writing), you are free to act in your own best interests with a free conscience. You are not an indentured servant no matter what bet was placed on you, and if someone is using guilt to influence your decisions, you can be sure they are acting in their best interests and not yours.

We've talked about what you owe the organization and the people you work for. But what do you owe the people who have come to work for you and with whom you've worked for years? Guess what? There're not really working for you—they're working for themselves. If they didn't believe that working for you was in their best interests, they'd be working somewhere else. You should respect people and treat them with dignity and consideration, but you're not their mother. You must do what's right for your career, just as everyone else must do what's right for their careers.

And don't get all moralistic on me here, because we've already established that you can't make yourself an Outstanding Success without making the people you work for and people who work for you successful along the way. But you shouldn't make your career decisions based on what's best for the careers of the people you work with any more than you should expect your boss or the people who work for you to make their career decisions based on what's best for you. If you manage your career according to the book's strategies and you become an Outstanding Success, you will make many people successful along the way—far more than if you sacrifice your success for some ostensible common good.

So your course is clear. You must think selfishly. You're getting paid to do what's best for the company, but that doesn't include sacrificing career opportunities. Other than doing the best possible job you can do for the people who hired you, and whatever else may be part of any legal agreements you've signed with the company, you owe it nothing. The company owes you whatever the people who hired you agreed to pay you and whatever else may be part of any legal agreements they've made with you. They owe you nothing else. This is true whether you've worked for the company for forty hours or forty years. It couldn't be simpler than that, and you should act accordingly.

How does all this work if you work in the public or nonprofit sectors, where the organization aspires to a higher purpose than merely making money for its owners? Say you work for a social services organization whose purpose is to help the homeless or for the public school system in an inner city whose purpose is to improve opportunities for the under-privileged. It could then happen that acting in your own interests, say, leaving for a better paying job in the private sector, may be bad for the homeless you're helping or the children of the underprivileged you're teaching.

As an employee of a nonprofit, you have to balance two of your own legitimate conflicting personal needs—to become successful, however you define that, and to help a group you strongly identify with. I've watched people in the military, in the intelligence services, in government, and in teaching go through this personal balancing act. For a long time, their personal need to help others wins out, sometimes lasting right through retirement. But often, spurred perhaps by the need to finance their children's educations or their own retirement, many conclude it's time to look after their personal financial needs.

The point is, again, that for the time you work for any given organization, you must take ownership and act as if you own it. But when the time comes to decide whether you should continue or move on, you should be driven by your own legitimate personal needs, among which may rightly be included a personal need to help others, and not by guilt or loyalty.

THE OUTSTANDING COMPANY

I have no doubt that many CEOs, venture capitalists, and investors will read this section on the selfish employee, shake their heads in consternation, and promise never to hire someone who selfishly puts himself ahead of the company he works for. These CEOs, venture capitalists, and investors would be wrong.

The most powerful company would be one where every employee was working to achieve Outstanding Success, where every employee was acting selfishly. Imagine it. Every employee is self-motivated—they chose to work for the organization because it allows them to stay on track to meet their career goals (strategy #1).

They all love what they're doing, they're really good at their jobs, and all feel the company and their jobs will lead them to achieve their personal goals (strategy #2).

They all work to maximize their personal career value by accumulating significant accomplishments (strategy #3), and they structure their jobs to deliver Outstanding Performance (strategy #4).

They manage their assignments to do what they say they're going to do (strategy #5). (This alone would qualify a company for the hall of fame.) All managers would make their bosses and the people who worked for them successful.

Finally, they would make decisions as if they owned 100% of the organization (strategy #6).

The CEOs, venture capitalists, and investors who would be the big losers are those running or investing in companies that don't make it possible for its employees to achieve Outstanding Success. These may be companies in bad industries, companies that are poorly run, or companies that don't give employees the support and freedom they need to achieve Outstanding Success. All the good, selfish people trying to achieve Outstanding Success would abandon these companies and their CEOs, venture capitalists, and investors.

With all the competent, selfish people gone, the poor companies and investments would soon fail. And the world would be a better place. While there may be discord between bad companies and selfish employees, there is absolutely no conflict between the selfish employee and the great company.

Let's say that so far you've followed this book's advice and you've done everything right. You've targeted a clear career goal, you're doing what you love and are good at, you're an outstanding performer, and you take a strong proprietary interest in your organization. There's only one person that can stop you now—you. And you do that if you self-destruct.

CHAPTER 7

OUTSTANDING SUCCESS STRATEGY #7

Don't Self–Destruct

In this chapter:

- Arrogance,
- Burning bridges,
- Discrimination,
- Dishonesty and self–dealing, and
- Inappropriate romantic affairs.

*The path to oblivion often goes through
a triumphal arch.*

DON-AMINADO, PSEUDONYM OF RUSSIAN AUTHOR
SHPOLANSKY AMINAD PETROVICH

ORGANIZATIONAL HYGIENE

Nothing in life is certain. You can execute diligently and competently all six of the strategies discussed in the preceding chapters and run into such a streak of bad luck that you still don't achieve Outstanding Success. Your company can fail or be acquired, your supporters can leave or even die at the wrong time, unexpected competition or new technologies can put your industry in the trash heap, or you can work for a series of start-ups that never fulfill their promise.

Still, it would take a great deal of bad luck over forty years for you not to succeed if you executed the six strategies of the previous chapters well. Even if you didn't make it into the top 1% of earners, it's still likely you'd be successful and happy for most of your career.

That is, unless you self-destruct. People self-destruct by not paying attention to what I call good organizational hygiene. Unlike the six strategies we've talked about up to now, good organizational hygiene will not necessarily contribute to your success directly. But ignoring it may well lead, at best, to being closed out of Outstanding Success. At worst, it can lead to your complete downfall and failure.

There is no end to things you can do so wrong that you ruin your career. Burst into your company's board of directors' meeting dressed like a duck, and your career is over no matter how much Outstanding Performance you've delivered during the past ten years. Or wind up on the front page, accused of committing some newsworthy felony. You may think of yourself as a superstar, but your name isn't going to come up again when HR is sorting through its top performer list.

But this isn't the type of bizarre behavior we're talking about. We're talking about behavior thoroughly rational people engage in with hardly a second thought, behavior that, perversely, is more likely to occur as a person becomes more successful. These behaviors are the five deadly sins in organizational life. Commit them and you may luck out and still achieve Outstanding Success, but you're playing Russian roulette with your career. Each time you transgress brings you closer to mediocrity or even utter ruin.

The behaviors you must avoid are:

- Arrogance

- Burning bridges

- Discrimination

- Dishonesty and self-dealing

- Inappropriate romantic affairs

Up to this point, every career strategy we've talked about is as important to the entry-level employee as it is to the CEO. This seventh strategy is different in that the better you are at executing on the first six strategies and the more successful you become, the more likely it is that you will self-destruct.

For a while, people may see arrogance in a young employee as confidence. In a senior executive, it's seen as disrespect. Burn a few bridges when you're young, and there may still be more bridges ahead. Do it when you're older, and you'll find yourself marooned. As you advance in your career and get more autonomy, you'll have greater opportunity for self-dealing and a record of good performance that may lead you to believe you have a right to more than you actually do.

Although the danger of self-destructing is greater as you become more senior, the habits of age are formed in youth, so don't skip this chapter just because you happen to be early in your career.

ARROGANCE

Arrogance is a strong feeling of proud self-importance that is expressed by treating other people with contempt or disregard. It is generally directed toward those below or at the same level as the arrogant person on the organization chart, though occasionally it extends to suppliers and customers as well. As long as you don't direct your arrogance upward, you may initially survive and even prosper in some organizations. Eventually, even senior people will tire of your rudeness to others, but for a while, they may reason that your behavior is just the cost of having someone as good as you doing whatever it is you do.

But arrogance is a terrible burden to carry if your objective is to achieve Outstanding Success. Sure, you might make it to the top in all your unexpurgated obnoxiousness, perhaps supported by a small cadre of cohorts you deem worthy, but the cards are stacked against you. If you should slip, have a bad spell, or need the support or extra effort of those on the receiving end of your arrogance, you'll suddenly find yourself isolated. And if things really start to go wrong, as they do from time to time for people striving to achieve Outstanding Success, you'll find those around you whose support you need the most tossing you anvils instead of life preservers.

Even if you don't stumble and your performance continues to be outstanding, if it comes at the expense of your support throughout the organization, even your senior management will eventually turn against you.

Neil was a certifiable genius, a crack systems developer who could design and program circles around the people he worked with. He was a gifted technician who was in the top 1% in productivity when it came to producing debugged, tight computer code. But he held all those around him in disdain, and in return he was universally disliked by his peers.

His productivity and genius made him a company asset, and his managers protected him from the rest of the firm and protected the customers from him. But despite their high regard for Neil, his managers would never promote him or give him the opportunity to become a leader in the company, a position he felt he deserved, especially, as he put it, "when compared to the baboons who were running the product development function."

Sadder still is the story of Sally, a brilliant lawyer who was an outstanding performer in a prestigious NYC firm for the eight grueling years it takes before you're considered for partnership. When her turn came, she was told, to her complete shock, that not only wouldn't she be made a partner, but she should find another job outside the firm.

Although her eight-year performance record had fully qualified her for partnership, she suffered one self-destructive problem—arrogance. The quality of her legal work was first class, but despite repeated warnings and coaching, she'd treat younger associates and supporting staff with disdain. She'd tell them they were stupid or incompetent and order them to do her bidding as if she was their intellectual superior and they were personal servants. The partners agreed that such behavior was bad for the firm irrespective of whatever other benefits she could bring to the partnership.

Arrogance is a dangerous drug. It provides a cheap high—an ego lift that comes from feeling superior to others and letting them know it. But over time, it will cause you to lose your support base, no matter how good or valuable you think you are. It's self-destructive behavior, so watch it!

BURNING BRIDGES

There is a type of person who goes through life believing that whom you know is more important than what you know. These people are very easy to dislike.

In point of fact, while whom you know is rarely more important than what you know, whom you know can still be important. On the positive side, people you know can open doors for you and give you opportunities, though it will be up to you to turn those opportunities into Outstanding Success. On the negative side, people who know you can stop you from becoming an Outstanding Success if they don't like you, believe in you, or trust you.

While many people who have achieved Outstanding Success are not particularly adept at networking, none burn bridges behind them, leaving a trail of hard feelings. Although it is occasionally difficult, they work hard to preserve their relationships and reputations with people they meet as they move along in their careers. While not everyone may love them, few people—past employers, past employees, vendors, competitors, customers, executive recruiters—dislike or disrespect them. There may be more than six billion people in the world, but if you wish to achieve Outstanding Success, it is best not to burn your bridges with any of them. The world of your career is remarkably small.

Lyle was a young salesman who quarreled with his manager about his commissions. In a fit of pique, he abruptly resigned without giving notice. Worse, he told his manager what he thought of him, calling him dishonest and stupid. As a final insult, he shared his feelings with friends he'd made at one of the firm's important prospects and cost the company a sale he and the company had been working on for almost a full year. Picture a burning bridge.

More than twenty years later, Lyle was the head of a management team trying to raise a desperately needed third round of venture capital for a high-tech start-up. As luck would have it, Lyle's old boss had become a partner in an important venture capital firm that was part of a group of venture capital firms that was close to providing Lyle's company financing. That is, until the deal came to the attention of Lyle's old boss, who advised his partners not to invest. When that firm pulled out at the last minute, the other firms asked why and Lyle's old boss told them. Two of the remaining firms then dropped out and the financing cratered. Lyle never figured out how things could go so wrong so quickly.

DISCRIMINATION

Competitors and the media have a field day whenever a politician or businessperson managing a public company says anything that offends someone, gleefully pouncing on the slightest faux pas and making it into a federal case (although, fairly, sometimes it actually is a federal case). When this happens, the person's career comes tumbling down like a building dynamited for demolition. There's noise, dust, and smoke everywhere for a few days as someone's career implodes in a heap.

Even if you don't have the stature to be press worthy, you're still not home free. One complaint to the right lawyer or government agency, and you'll be spending a good portion of your income and time getting a firsthand look at the wrong side of the legal system.

I would hope that everyone sees the overall benefit to antidiscrimination and sexual harassment laws. But even if you do not, you must accept today's reality and adopt a zero-tolerance policy to even the slightest hint of discrimination, bigotry, or sexual harassment.

Certainly that means you must not take actions, express opinions, or make comments that can in any way be perceived as discriminatory, bigoted, or sexually inappropriate. But more than that, you should not tolerate even the most subtle prejudiced attitudes, even down to wisecracks, innuendos, or offhand comments. And this includes even among your most trusted friends and colleagues in the most private of moments. One slip and you may be seen as untrustworthy or secretly bigoted. It's the third rail that will destroy your career if you give it even the slightest brush.

A quintessential example of this might be Earl Butz, who was secretary of agriculture under President Gerald Ford. In a severely misguided effort to be funny, he told a dirty joke and made a racist comment in front of other prominent white males one can only guess he felt shared his bawdy sense of humor and lack of respect for African-Americans. Apparently, they did not. The response started slowly but soon became headlines, and his career was instantly over. The only good that came from this was that he had it coming to him. (Perhaps working to solidify his reputation, Butz later pleaded guilty to tax evasion and was sentenced to fines and imprisonment.)

Thirty-one years later, Don Imus, the legendary radio personality, made what he felt was a casual, harmless, clever, offhand sexist and racist remark during his early morning radio show. In less than two weeks his career was derailed as he lost his sponsors and his nationally syndicated radio and television shows. Like Earl Butz, he self-destructed and learned the hard way that there is no such thing as a harmless racist or sexist remark.

If you don't like this loss of freedom to speak your mind or have a different opinion, too bad. You're free to hold whatever opinion you please and, for the most part, express it in any forum. But if you choose to do so, the cost will be that you will not achieve Outstanding Success. Of course it is best if you are intolerant of sexual harassment or discrimination toward any group because you sincerely believe in every fiber of your being that it is the right thing to do. But if that connection was somehow never created within you, do it so that one day when your guard is down you don't self-destruct.

DISHONESTY AND
SELF-DEALING

People do things for one reason and one reason only: to fulfill their personal needs. Even when they're fulfilling the personal needs of someone else—their family, friends, or colleagues—they're fulfilling a personal need to fulfill someone else's personal needs. So everyone, to some extent, is out for himself or herself.

Deep down, everyone knows this and not only accepts this behavior in others, but expects it. It is the fundamental assumption behind every incentive and compensation plan ever devised. But when you are part of an organization, there are unspoken rules that limit this behavior, and if someone is caught breaching these limits, he's tossed out on his ear.

Because every organization and situation is different, it's impossible to provide concrete guidance on exactly where the line is drawn between acceptable self-interest and unacceptable self-dealing. For example, what is normal compensation in big-time investment banking is far different from what is normal in the nonprofit sector. But as Justice Potter Stewart said about pornography, "I know it when I see it," people know when they see self-dealing going beyond acceptable limits.

Of course there are examples of people breaking the law for their own gain—from CEOs who cook the books to keep their company's stock price high, to salespeople who stuff channels or make secret agreements with customers that make it appear as if they've achieved sales levels necessary to collect unearned commissions, to ordinary employees who cheat on their expense reports. But what trips people up more often is self-dealing that is not illegal, but that transcends unspoken tradition or that is outside the norms for a particular company or industry.

Consider the well-publicized case of Richard Grasso, a past CEO of the New York Stock Exchange. Grasso is a college dropout who began work at the NYSE in 1967 as a floor clerk earning $82.50 a week. There is no disputing that he was an effective leader, rising to become the exchange's CEO, providing the organization deft leadership, and greatly increasing its value and standing. But what compensation should he have received for his unquestioned significant contribution?

The NYSE was a nonprofit organization, and it is well understood that in the nonprofit sector executive compensation is always modest. But Grasso felt he should be paid more in line with the people who headed the companies his organization served, and he persuaded his board of directors to award him a pay package widely reported in the press to be $140–$180 million (depending on who was doing the addition).

Whether Grasso, or any single individual, is worth $140 million is not the issue. The issue is that Grasso's compensation was out of line with what the world had come to expect for CEOs of nonprofit organizations. By crossing the line between looking out for his own best interests and unreasonable self-dealing, he self-destructed. He lost his job, and the government sued him to return a large portion of his earnings.

It is easy for most people to think that $140 million could only represent greed that is beyond the pale, and that they'd never let themselves reach such a situation. But people do it all the time—stretching the envelope when it comes to lunch and dinner expenses, dry cleaning in hotels, overuse of taxis and car services, too many golf outings at the most exclusive and costly clubs.

Consider June, a young, highly competent financial analyst being recruited by an elite nonprofit to be the group's controller. June was working at a commercial bank and was paid fairly but modestly. The new job would represent a significant promotion and was a much more exciting position, but she knew the person she was being recruited to replace earned three times her compensation at the bank.

The firm recruiting June liked her intelligence, high energy, experience, and that she was a minority female. They offered her an 80% increase in target compensation, far more than most people can expect when changing jobs. June loved the opportunity and the people, but yet she held out in an effort to get the organization to pay her an amount closer to the earnings of the person she was replacing. It is not that she didn't believe an 80% increase wasn't very generous, but she wanted more simply because someone else had earned more.

Here was a midcareer person doing on a small scale what Grasso did so publicly on a large scale—she was pushing beyond the perceived norm to a point of perceived greediness. This was an unprecedented opportunity for her to take a large step toward achieving Outstanding Success, and she was about to self-destruct. Fortunately, a good friend was advising her and set her straight, but had June followed her own self-destructive instincts, she would have set her career back a decade.

INAPPROPRIATE ROMANTIC AFFAIRS

Let's face the facts. Men and women with careers are at work for the greater part of their waking hours, which makes meeting potential romantic partners outside work very difficult. Moreover, chemistry often happens when people work closely together for long periods, sharing common goals, aspirations, and experiences.

I don't know the statistics, but it's certain that many children would not be on the earth today if it weren't for at-work romances and marriages. But with all that said, office romance and your job are a volatile mixture that can blow up a promising career or even lead to sexual harassment lawsuits.

Terry was a divorced senior executive beloved in his company and by its founder, and was in line to be the next CEO of this rapidly growing, publicly traded company. But he had a passionate affair with a married woman high up in middle management. The woman's husband learned of the affair, complained to the company's CEO, and threatened to make a fuss.

Despite Terry's standing within the company, his career there was finished. It did not matter that Terry was not married at the time of the affair, or that the woman did not report directly or indirectly to Terry and he had no influence over her career or compensation. The affair threatened to cause a scandal the founder felt his high-visibility public company could not tolerate, and he decided he had no choice but to ask Terry to leave. Terry eventually recovered his career momentum, but the incident set him back significantly in both time and level of success.

I refer to this example, because it illustrates the murkiness of this topic. There was no implication of sexual harassment; this was just one of those natural loving relationships. It happens. It can happen to you.

But your career is not high school. To get to the point Terry reached in his relationship, one thing had to lead to another. He could have stopped the sequence early on and avoided the eventual embarrassment for him, the woman, and the company. Whether his life would have been better or worse for resisting the affair is difficult to say. But if achieving Outstanding Success is an overriding objective, discretion is generally the safest option as the importance, visibility, and seniority of your position increases.

With this said, there are many people who survive an inappropriate romantic relationship. There may be much Sturm und Drang, and perhaps some embarrassment for a while, and maybe there's a messy divorce and someone loses half his stuff. But depending on how important the individuals are to the organization's success, the ethos of the organization, and the milieu in which it operates, the careers may survive relatively intact. Nevertheless, have an inappropriate romantic affair, and you're playing with fire. To a large extent, this is the bet you make. Life and love are often more important than a mere career, but sometimes love can appear to be tawdry in the harsh light of day. If something goes wrong along the way, something that may have nothing to do with your affair, the embarrassing details suddenly come front and center for all the world to use against you. You suddenly and painfully learn you haven't survived the inappropriate relationship after all.

You must decide the circumstances and the price you're willing to pay. But remember, if you can't do the time, don't do the crime. If you allow yourself to be governed by your heart or your hormones and self-destruct due to an inappropriate affair, don't say you haven't been warned.

There you have it—arrogance, burning bridges, discrimination, self-dealing, and inappropriate romantic affairs. There are a lot of other things you can do wrong, but most won't destroy your career. These are the five that sneak up on otherwise intelligent, successful people and lead to a ruined career. They are insidious because successful people know they are unlikely to suffer any cost due to a single transgression. Treat one person with disdain, forge one receipt for your expense report, make one bigoted joke, have a quick fling after the holiday party—no single act is likely to bring you down. But like rust that corrodes the strongest iron ship, these behaviors accumulate over time to sink your career. And you can never tell which mistake may be the one that changes your life from promising to pitiful. So steer clear if your goal is to achieve Outstanding Success.

Be a Heat-Seeking Missile, work in your Outstanding Success Zone, maximize your career value, swing for the bleachers by always working in jobs were you can deliver Outstanding Performance, deliver the goods, take ownership, and don't self-destruct. If you follow these seven strategies, there's a good chance you'll achieve Outstanding Success. All you have to do is put these strategies into practice in the real world, which is the topic of part II.

PART II

PUTTING STRATEGIES INTO PRACTICE

For one person who dreams of earning fifty thousand pounds, a hundred people dream of being left fifty thousand pounds.

A. A. Milne

CHAPTER 8

COACH YOURSELF

In this chapter:

How to put the seven Outstanding Success strategies into practice in your real-world life.

You cannot teach a man anything; you can only help him find it within himself.

GALILEO

HAMLET VS. BEAVIS AND BUTT-HEAD

Whether you're flying an airplane, raising children, or managing your career, it's never as straightforward and easy to do as the instruction books make it seem. While you may have studied diligently, the real world hasn't read the book and fails to act according to the script. There you are, trying to play *Hamlet* while the real world is doing *Beavis and Butt-Head*.

Nevertheless, having coached people through difficult parts of their careers, I've learned that the most unpredictable element in the career management equation is not the real world. It's you.

Tell people how to get on a different career track more likely to lead to Outstanding Success, and instead of finding ways to change, they tend to find ironclad excuses why they can't change. After basking in the personal attention that comes from being coached, people too often simply fall back into their precoaching work patterns. As someone I once worked for used to say, "They jump up and down, generate lots of heat and smoke but no forward motion." They metaphorically slap their foreheads, thank me for the brilliant insights, then proceed to change nothing.

Worried about the effectiveness of this entire concept of career coaching, I talked with someone with extensive career coaching experience. She told me this was far more usual than unusual. She found that whenever she coached clients who were unemployed and looking for jobs, they generally followed the tactical advice she gave them, such as how to improve their résumés, conduct themselves in an interview, or handle a difficult boss. But if they were employed with a paycheck coming in, they rarely followed career strategic advice that would, over time, bring more lasting benefits.

This was as troubling to her as it was to me, but she pointed out that physicians, personal fitness coaches, and other personal advisers share this experience. That is, clients follow tactical advice to fix an immediate and pressing problem, but ignore life-altering strategic advice that can eliminate the source of the problem entirely.

I got to thinking about a good friend who had had a heart attack. During his recovery he ate a strictly healthy diet, lost weight, and exercised. But once the immediate danger passed, he was back to the habits that led to the heart attack in the first place. So my career coaching friend's observation rang true and piqued my interest.

SIDE EFFECTS

I didn't know of any studies done including clients of personal trainers or career coaches, but a lot of work has been done tracking the behavior of physicians' patients. So I did some research, and what I found about people who visited doctors squared with what I was finding about those looking for career guidance.

Oversimplifying somewhat—but not much—most people don't follow the advice they seek out and are given, even when it's given by professionals they trust and believe in. For example, one study found that 75% of patients don't take their medications as prescribed. Another study found that one in three Americans never take any of their prescribed medications at all. Tony Zook, then president and CEO of AstraZeneca US, in remarks at the World Healthcare Innovation and Technology Congress in 2006, reported, "It is estimated that 125,00 people with treatable ailments die each year simply because they do not take prescribed medications properly or they skip them altogether."

But he provided me special insight into the underlying human dynamic when he asked, "What exactly does the world expect from a pharmaceutical company?" His answer:

- They want a single pill to meet an unmet need.

- They want it to immediately improve a condition.

- They don't want side effects.

- They want it to be inexpensive.

Unfortunately, most medications for serious illnesses don't work this way. The cure for many maladies involves multiple medications taken over an extended period. Worse, many medications have side effects, some of which are profound. Moreover, the solution to many health problems requires changes in personal habits, such as diet, exercise, and stress reduction.

This is clearly not the kind of simple solution most people are looking for, so as soon as the immediate health threat seems to retreat, people ignore their doctor's advice and go back to their old ways.

The parallel with career coaching is astonishing. Making a few modifications to account for the difference between medicinal prescriptions and career prescriptions, here is what people want from a solution to their career problems:

- A single, simple solution that will solve all their career problems.

- They want it to immediately improve their career.

- And especially, they don't want any side effects. Here, "side effects" means they don't want the solution to affect their lives in any negative way, such as causing them to experience change or increased risk.

Unfortunately, when it comes to improving your career prospects, there is rarely such a solution. Don't expect that you can go to work on Monday and do one simple thing differently. Nor will things change by Friday of the same week. You can't get into good physical condition in one week if Cheetos has been a major food group for you for the past few years and you consider text messaging to be aerobic exercise. Similarly, there's nothing you can do that will dramatically improve your career in a single week, a single month, or possibly even a single year if all you've done to manage your career for years is dress for work every morning, show up, and do your job.

Finally, if you begin to manage your career with unwavering purpose, there's a good chance there will be side effects, some significant.

Herb was a detective whose chief thought he was too valuable in his current job to promote. There wasn't any solution to this demoralizing career problem that didn't have side effects. If he confronted the chief, he'd risk retribution. If he moved to a new department in a new town, he'd have to relocate his family. If he moved into the private sector, he'd forfeit unvested pension benefits and risk that things might not go well in his new job. These are all major side effects.

The result: Herb sucked it up and continued to work in a job that didn't allow him to achieve his potential. He knew what he had to do, but his fear of possible side effects kept him stuck in a career rut, doomed to have no chance of being happy with his work, much less achieving Outstanding Success.

Ralph was the successful CIO of a major industrial company, but he correctly sensed he'd gone as high as he could in the company. He needed to immerse himself in the business details of his company and his company's industry to understand how information technology could transform his company and help bring it to a new level. This was not a fast, simple solution with no side effects.

Ralph was an engineer, and he was reluctant to move outside his comfort zone of technology to deal with less structured business issues. So he continued to devote his energies, and the resources under his management, to classic nonstrategic tasks—installing and running servers, building support systems, converting database management systems. All part of his job, and tasks that as an engineer he found interesting. But he was doing nothing that would take him to the next level in the company. He left his career prescription on the shelf and continued with a strategy that was almost sure to land him among the Forlorn.

Career coaching at the strategic level is a communication-intensive process structured around questions designed to help both the client and the coach understand the issues, opportunities, and roadblocks in a client's career. Because every individual and every career is different, the coaching process must be customized to account for each client's unique circumstances and experiences.

Nevertheless, based on the seven Outstanding Success strategies, coaching and questioning move in a predictable direction. But the only person who can really make your career more successful is you. *You* must figure out how to manage your career, *you* must develop an action plan, and *you* must execute that plan.

Remember all those people who visit physicians and then don't take their advice? Remember all those people who don't exercise or eat right, even though they know they should? Don't become one of those people when it comes to your career. You have it in your power to change your life for the better, though it will take time and there may be side effects.

We begin with finding your Heat-Seeking Missile target.

BECOME A HEAT-SEEKING MISSILE

I asked a young marine captain what his career objective was in the marines. His answer: "To stay in as long as I'm having fun."

That is not the kind of objective that can guide your career. That's classic drifting. "Why not," I asked him, "set becoming a general as your career objective? Among your colleagues are marine captains who are your age who will someday become generals. There is no reason you can't be one of them. If the journey from captain to general stops being fun, you can always leave, so you haven't sacrificed anything by committing to a worthy career target. But if you continue focusing just on having fun and not where having fun can take you, the chance that you will someday become a general is very low."

You may not be a marine, but setting your sights on a target that is both worthy and achievable is your first self-coaching task in managing your career. This is a deceptively difficult job for many people. If you look out far enough, there are many things you can realistically aspire to achieve that may seem far out of reach today. For example, we talked about Lewis Ranieri in a previous chapter; he began working in the mailroom of a major Wall Street firm as a college dropout and rose to become vice chairman of the firm, a major force in the financial services industry, and a very wealthy man.

As you get older, your realistic options decrease, but with enough time left in the future, you can still move far from where you are today. So if you really want to be a general, the CEO of a Fortune 500 company, or a senator, that's fine. It's okay to err on the high side as long as you're not utterly unrealistic and as long as you're willing to change your life today in an effort to achieve what you say you want. To be sure you're aiming at a realistic Heat-Seeking Missile target, you should focus not solely on your ultimate goal, but also on intermediate goals you have to meet to get you there. Toward this end, it is generally easier if you work backward from retirement to where you are today. Specifically, write down where you want to be:

1. When you retire

2. In ten years

3. In five years

4. This time next year

5. This time three months from today

6. Finally, succinctly describe exactly where you are today

Don't just talk about what you want to achieve—write it down. This is important so you know your thinking is clear (nothing is so effective at exposing a harebrained idea for what it is as writing it down) and so you have something you can refer back to over time.

If you're less than ten years from retirement, answer as many of these as you have years left to work. Start backward from the future, because we want everything you do to be directed toward your Heat-Seeking Missile target. Creating such a list helps ensure a realistic progression from where you are now to where you eventually want to be.

When you think you know what you want to achieve and you've written it down, post it somewhere you can see it every day. Looking every day at what you've written will serve one of three purposes:

- **Reinforcement.** The list will serve to keep you motivated and on track.

- **A "What was I thinking?" alert.** There's a good chance that despite your best efforts you won't get your targeting right the first time around. Or even the second or third. You thought you wanted to become a medical researcher but hated molecular biology. You were targeting a life defending the poor but can't live on a public defender's salary. Looking every day at the targets you set will alert you to the need to redo the exercise.

· **A diversion alert.** You may have chosen a worthy, realistic, and desirable target, but reality is getting in the way. The company you work for isn't growing, your party lost the election, you're spending so much time commuting that your life and work are suffering. For whatever reason, you're being diverted from your goal. Having your goals in front of you every day alerts you to the need to create a new reality if you're really serious about achieving Outstanding Success.

The next step is to ensure that there is a realistic path from where you are today to where you want to be in the future. To help you with that, begin with where you are today and work your way forward. Specifically, answer the following question: What is it I have to do to move from where I am today to where I want to be in three months?

Be very specific. For example, "Learn more about the business" is not specific. "Transfer to the sales department" is more specific. "Reduce my living expenses so I'm not stuck working in a job I hate" is not specific. "Trade the Mercedes for a Chevy and pay off my high credit card debt with the proceeds of a second mortgage so I can afford to start over in a different field" is more specific.

Then answer the question "Assuming I'm successful in moving to where I want to be in three months, what do I have to do to move to where I want to be in one year?" Next, answer the question "Assuming I'm successful in moving to where I want to be in one year, what do I have to do to move to where I want to be in five years?" Finally, answer the question "Assuming I'm successful in moving to where I want to be in five years, what do I have to do to move to where I want to be in ten years?"

Once you have written down your answers to these questions, you come to the most important question of all: "What do I have to do *starting today* if I hope to move from where I am to where I want to be in three months, in one year, in five years, and in ten years?" Again, write down the answer.

At this point you may find, or think you find, things that are stopping you from doing today what you have to do if you hope to move forward. You have to quit work and go back to school, but you have financial obligations. You have to leave the company to find another job, but that would mean leaving fifteen years of pension vesting. You should move to another organization where there are more opportunities, but that would mean relocating the children to another school.

These are the side effects of taking your prescription for achieving Outstanding Success. Some of these side effects may be scary—relocation, increased risk, loss of seniority, loss of security, hard work, increased schooling, and so forth. And there's no guarantee of success, even if you suffer the side effects.

There is no end of reasons not to do what you should do to move from where you are to where you say want to be. But this is the litmus test. If you allow any of these reasons to stop you, however legitimate you've convinced yourself these reasons are, or if you persuade yourself you just need more time before you take action, it's almost certain you will not achieve Outstanding Success.

The coming year, wherever that year happens to be in your career and however old you are, is a critically important time if you hope to achieve Outstanding Success. If you don't begin taking decisive action today, you will find yourself no closer to your goal one year from today than you are today. But if you act on your plans, you'll be surprised how dramatically your career changes as the years go by.

FINDING THE ZONE

Committing to a worthy career target is fine, but how do you know you've chosen a path that's right for you? Becoming a marine general, a CEO, or the superintendent of New York City's schools may be exciting Outstanding Success career targets, but not if you wind up hating your job or if you're shooting for a job that for some reason you're just not good enough to get.

There are three approaches to finding your Outstanding Success Zone:

- Searching,

- Focusing first on what makes you happy and you're good at, or

- Focusing first on where you want to end up.

With the searching approach, you move from job to job until something clicks—until you find yourself succeeding and loving what you do. As undisciplined and random as this sounds, it works for people who have no idea what they want to do or what they're good at.

Lynn, who we met briefly in chapter 2, started college as an English major, based on her successful experiences in the liberal arts in high school. But as she took more advanced English and literature courses, her practical nature led her to believe that studying English would not lead her to a position of both intellectual interest and financial security.

A friend suggested she take an economics course, which she did. Lynn loved the combination of the rigor of economics and its practical use in society, so she switched majors and graduated first in her class in economics. She received a full fellowship to study economics at one of the country's top graduate schools and accepted. But after her first year Lynn found the minutiae of economics less and less interesting. So she looked for what else might be more interesting and applied to politics. Again she was accepted at a graduate school with a full fellowship, but she again lost interest after a year.

Lynn then left school and joined a financial services firm and quickly became one of their top young stars. But she found the work lacked intellectual challenge and after less than a year applied to law school. Finally, after five tries, she found her place. She loved the law and excelled. She graduated high in her class, clerked in the federal district courts, joined a prestigious New York City law firm, and became one of the firm's first women partners and an Outstanding Success.

Lynn moved from job to job in a directed fashion. That is, she didn't allow herself to be diverted by her success into doing something she didn't enjoy or that she enjoyed but that didn't allow her to achieve her financial objectives. Most people are not this disciplined, and they stop their search before they find their Outstanding Success Zone or they change jobs more to escape from what they don't like than to find what they do like. If you select this trial-and-error method of finding your Outstanding Success Zone, you must be careful to always change with purpose and direction.

The second approach to finding your Outstanding Success Zone works best if you know what you love to do and are really, really good at. Holding that constant, you then look for what you can do that will meet your personal objectives.

My son has had a decade-long love of music. He began playing the guitar, then the bagpipes (!), then drums, bass, piano, and sitar. He's recently added a clarinet and flute to his repertoire and is negotiating with a friend to trade an old guitar for a saxophone. He never met an instrument he hasn't wanted to learn to play. Additionally, he sings, writes music and lyrics, and records. Although he enjoyed and participated in sports and drama, he was passionate about hard rock music. He formed bands and performed at every opportunity. He wrote original music and recorded entire albums, both with others and single-handedly.

Here's what I know about music, and the hard rock genre in particular: it's a really tough way to earn a living. My son agrees and is realistic and concerned but not deterred. He knows what he loves and what he's good at. He wants a well-rounded education, so in college he's studying liberal arts, taking courses in everything from accounting, economics, and chemistry, to art history and Asian history. But he's clear on his professional objectives. He is intent on finding a career in music that will lead to financial success as well as to creative fulfillment.

While I do not envy him his search, I am watching a classic example of someone who starts with what he wants to do and is good at and looks for a way to turn it into a successful career. It is an example of how knowing what you want to do can be both a blessing and a curse.

While this approach of starting from what you love to do is certainly viable, it requires something few people have—a knowledge of what they really want to do for the forty years of their career. If this were the only approach to finding a career, there would likely be few accountants, salespeople, or advertising executives in the world, just to pick a few career paths at random. Few children wake up one morning and decide they really have the same burning passion for accounting, sales, or advertising that my son has for music.

Instead, most jobs are acquired tastes, and we need an approach to finding your Outstanding Success Zone that takes into account the fact that most people discover indirectly what they love to do and are good at. Which leads to the third approach to finding your Outstanding Success Zone.

In this third approach, which is far more common in Career World, you:

- First take a shot on targeting where you want to wind up in your career,

- Then you determine what you have to do to get there, and finally,

· Ask yourself if you realistically have the ability to do what has to be done and if you'd enjoy the trip. If not, you go back to step one and rethink your career target with greater insight into what works for you—what will put you in your Outstanding Success Zone.

In chapter 2 we talked about Hank, who made a career for himself in employee benefits. We can be confident that as a young boy in grade school, Hank didn't announce to his parents over the breakfast table that he really wanted to work in employee benefits when he grew up. Receiving only a single job offer after college, he was forced to work in employee benefits. But he knew he wanted to run his own business, and he saw a way he could do that in employee benefits. He figured out what he had to do to achieve his goal and discovered that it was something he could become really good at and that he enjoyed doing. Mission accomplished—he found his Outstanding Success Zone and went on to become an Outstanding Success.

MAXIMIZE YOUR VALUE

Now you've got a long-term career target, a series of steps to reach it, and you're confident you'll be in your Outstanding Success Zone. Besides increasing how happy you are in your work, you're on your way to a career that will pay you more money. Exactly how much you're paid will be influenced by what you accomplish, but as we said in chapter 3, that's not the whole story.

Whether through policy or simple budget realities, many organizations pay far, far less than others for the same work and the same accomplishments. The disparity in total compensation, whether it's in the job of CEO, CIO, teacher, or police chief, can be 50% to more than 500%. If you work in rural Mississippi your earnings potential is far less than if you work in rural Massachusetts, which is less than if you work in Boston, no matter what you do for a living. Work in the public sector pays far less than equivalent work and performance in the private sector. Some industries, like manufacturing, typically pay less than others, like financial services. So it's time to make some decisions and face up to possible side effects.

Specifically, at issue is the trade-off between career success and the quality of life that may be associated with lower-paying positions—you may be able to trade that high-power job for one with lower career potential but with a shorter commute, more reasonable working hours, and with the option of living in a part of the country with lower cost of housing.

But sometimes the benefits are not all they seem to be. Is it really worth a thirty-minute shorter commute if you're earning 50% less than you're really worth? Are your children really better off having a larger lawn to play on than they would be if they were receiving the first-class public education only a well-funded school district can provide? Are you really going to be happy and fulfill your potential if you always opt to work for organizations where you can live near your parents or boyfriend or girlfriend but your total lifetime earnings will be a fraction of what they'd be if you made a few personal sacrifices?

The answers to these questions are very personal, but you must understand the trade-offs you may be making between achieving Outstanding Success in your career and improvements in your lifestyle. Achieving Outstanding

Success sometimes requires time away from home travel-ing, relocations in response to promotions, not being able to attend all the kids' soccer games, a parent who's occa-sionally exhausted trying to balance family and work lives. But the benefits in personal happiness, financial success, and opportunities for children can be enormous.

Of course it's a Pyrrhic victory to sacrifice your per-sonal and family happiness to career success. But just as career success sometimes comes at too high a price in an individual's quality of life, there are also quality-of-life improvements that come at far too high a price paid in career success. The choice is yours. It's much easier to live with the consequences, one way or the other, if you've made the choice with great thought and consideration.

Once you settle on this trade-off between work and other life issues, there's still the important decision regarding what job you should take. It helps if you see all jobs as fall-ing into one of three categories:

- Jobs in which you are assigned to do things—build systems, make sales, close the books, walk a beat, teach a class.

- Jobs where you are given an objective and are ex-pected to figure out how to accomplish it—increase sales, improve students' test scores, use information technology to decrease costs.

- Jobs where you must figure out what objectives need to be achieved to help the organization you work for.

These job categories form an ascending hierarchy, but they are not independent. That is, if your job is to figure out how to achieve objectives you're given, you must both develop a plan for achieving the objectives and deliver those objectives according to your plan. If you're in a job where you first have to figure out what the objectives should be, you must do that, then develop a plan for achieving those objectives, and then see to it that the objectives are achieved.

If you want to maximize your value, you must understand that there is an order of magnitude difference in value between each of these different levels. You should always work to be in jobs where you are in the top category. And that goes from early on in your career right through to retirement.

In chapter 4 we learned about Eliot, who was hired at nineteen to do some of the worst jobs in the factory of a company that manufactured electric motors. He was hired at the lowest level (to do stuff), but he quickly moved to the top level (figure out what should be done). He single-handedly took over the factory rework problem by figuring out what had to be done to make the company more successful (the top level), creating a process for fixing quality problems (the second level), and then actually fixing the problems (the lowest level). Had someone else figured out what had to be done and how it should be done and assigned the work to Eliot, Eliot would have been just another worker bee.

SWING FOR THE BLEACHERS

It's a mistake to assume you'll have to quit your job and change careers if you want to achieve Outstanding Success. In fact, the easiest place to begin working toward achieving Outstanding Success is in the job you currently have. But you have to stop being bound by your job description, and you have to stop depending on your boss to make you successful.

This is the time to ask the key question posed in chapter 4: What is it I can do in my job that my boss and other higher levels of management would consider to be absolutely Outstanding Performance? Remember, we're not talking about employee-of-the-month performance rewarded with a plaque or a month of parking next to the CEO near the front of the building. We're describing performance about which your management would shout from the rooftops.

Interestingly, it is in applying this fourth strategy where coaching often proves most helpful. People are too ready to blame their jobs, their bosses, and the organization they work for generally for not being able to get ahead. In fact, very often people hold themselves back because they see constraints that don't really exist. "I can't do that because that's not my job" or "My boss would never approve of that" is how they think. What they should be thinking is, "How do I change my job so I make my boss (and myself) wildly successful?" If you can answer that question, no boss will hold you back.

So study your organization and understand what you can do to deliver Outstanding Performance. If there is really nothing you can do, you have to move on. But if you think outside the margins of your job description and find what you can do that would be seen as truly Outstanding Performance, you can immediately begin to move forward toward achieving Outstanding Success at virtually no cost to you.

DELIVER THE GOODS

Once you've settled on what you're going to do to deliver Outstanding Performance, you must manage yourself and whatever resources you're assigned to do what you say you're going to do. As we said in chapter 5, by far the most important aspect of this is to focus all your time, energy, and resources on doing only those things that will result in your delivering Outstanding Performance or avoiding an Outstanding Failure.

But if you decide to do this on Friday and go to work on Monday without a specific plan, you will almost certainly fail. The normal forces of the organization will pull you in dozens of unproductive directions (from the standpoint of your delivering Outstanding Performance). You need a structured, disciplined, highly goal-directed approach to managing yourself and, if you're a manager, the people who work for you. I have found the following simple process to be very effective.

First, decide those few things you can do over the course of one or more years that would be considered Outstanding Performance. There may be only one thing that rises to the level of Outstanding Performance, but there should certainly not be more than three or four, and then only if you're very senior in the organization and manage a lot of people. Write a description of these things, which I call Outstanding Performance Possibilities. This very short list should change very slowly from year to year (unless you move into a new job).

For example, if you're a sales manager, perhaps the two long-term accomplishments the entire firm would clearly feel represented Outstanding Performance might be to increase sales by 40% per year and to displace your primary competitor in large accounts. If you are a systems manager, your Outstanding Performance Possibility might be to develop a system that reduces the cost of filling orders by 50% while delivering industry-leading customer satisfaction. If you're a teacher, your Outstanding Performance Possibility might be to raise the math SAT scores in your class so they are a hundred points ahead of the rest of the school district.

But these are ambitious objectives you're unlikely to accomplish in a single month, quarter, or even a year. So for each of your Outstanding Performance Possibilities, you must figure out, and write down, precisely what you will do in the next three months that will move you toward achieving these objectives. These are your short-term deliverables. They change from month to month or quarter to quarter, and accumulate over time to lead to Outstanding Performance. By forcing this short-interval discipline upon yourself, you ensure that you know exactly how you should be spending your time in the short run if you hope to achieve long-run success.

So let's look at our teacher who hopes to raise the average math SAT scores of her students by a hundred points. If her plan is to simply continue to teach as best as she can, it's more than likely she will not come near succeeding in her Outstanding Performance goal. So she analyzes the challenge and realizes that she can achieve her goal only if both the students and their parents see the benefit and agree to sign up for what is sure to be an intensive program of learning. Moreover, she understands that students will require better workbooks than the school can afford, and that many students will need one-on-one tutoring she cannot provide by herself.

The challenge is daunting, but there's a solution to every problem, though none is provided through the conventional school channels. For example, one of her deliverables may be to enlist the older, better students to tutor the younger, slower students, making it a point of pride to earn the status of tutor. So for six months the teacher organizes her lesson plan around creating a student tutoring program. This takes time, but once it's done, she's taken an important step toward delivering Outstanding Performance. But there's still a long way to go.

Because she needs additional teaching material the school cannot provide, the teacher sets as another deliverable to find two or three local businesses that will donate the money she needs to buy supplies. During parent-teacher meetings, she asks parents who can afford it to help provide their children with materials they'll need. This becomes her focus for another three months.

Note that none of this is part of the teacher's job description. Nor does any of it really require her principal's involvement or even approval. It may take her several years to achieve her goal, but she has set deliverables for every term so she knows she's making progress toward her Outstanding Performance objectives. She focuses all her energies on the deliverables she's set for herself, doing just enough of the administrative work the school requires of her to stay employed.

I have used this structured, disciplined approach to manage every department and company I have ever run. It has contributed to my personal success almost more than any other factor. Many people who worked for me found it so effective and motivating, they continued to use the same approach throughout their careers. It was a process I developed on my own and never asked permission to use.

Although I used this approach for decades in many different companies, I never once explicitly cleared the deliverables the people working for me were trying to achieve with the management of whatever company I happened to work for. More often than not, the people I worked for were entirely unaware, and even uninterested in, the periodic deliverables I set or the process I used to achieve them. They cared only about the end results.

I say this so readers understand that they do not have to look to their managers to provide them leadership. They can take the reins and provide leadership themselves. The result will be a constant movement toward Outstanding Success for yourself, the people who work for you, and the people you work for. Unless your organization is truly dysfunctional (which we'll talk about in the next chapter), no one will stop you. You will become an Outstanding Success.

SUMMING UP

If you are not already on the road to achieving Outstanding Success, you can make things better if you take a structured approach to applying the Outstanding Success strategies. That means thinking through your opportunities, identifying challenges, and developing a continuing series of short-term deliverables that will lead to Outstanding Performance. Specifically, write out where you want to be:

- When you retire

- In ten years

- In five years

- This time next year

- This time three months from today

- Finally, where you are today

But most importantly, you must have the will and fortitude to follow your own plan. While you should begin to take action as soon as possible, there is rarely an overnight solution, and it often comes with some side effects.

The scary part is that your success is entirely in your hands. The exciting part is that your success is entirely in your hands.

CHAPTER 9

STRATEGIES
for an
IMPERFECT WORLD

In this chapter, how to deal with an organization that has one to three types of career dysfunction:

- Dysfunctional strategy
- Dysfunctional management
- Dysfunctional behavior

Never play down the importance of incompetence in the organization. It has always been the seed of discontent, independence and successful entrepreneurship.

WILLIAM BLISS

MY BOSS IS A JERK

As you read through the strategies for achieving Outstanding Success, you may think, "This all sounds fine except for one thing. My boss is a jerk." This message, in one form or another, at times more muffled and at times even far more critical, is one career coaches, spouses, and bartenders hear often.

It can be a valid point, as careers take place in an imperfect world where you may encounter or even be surrounded by imperfect people. If you find yourself in such a situation, don't despair. Depending on the nature of your boss's shortcomings, the fact that your boss is ineffective or incompetent may be the best thing that can happen to your career. But being realistic, it might also be the worst. Because the outcome depends on the specifics of the situation, we're going to examine the different types of career dysfunctions you may encounter in your working life, and discuss what you should do about dysfunction when you encounter it.

In the context of your career, dysfunction means a consistent pattern of behavior within the organization that prevents you from succeeding even when you're doing everything right. The three types of dysfunction you might encounter at different times in your career, sometimes separately and sometimes together, are:

- Dysfunctional strategy
- Dysfunctional management
- Dysfunctional behavior

We'll talk about each of these three distinct types of dysfunction, but we first need some balance and perspective.

Despite *Dilbert* cartoons and Hollywood's penchant for depicting the working world as full of borderline sociopaths and dysfunctional managers, it's not that way at all. For the most part it's full of reasonably smart, normal people who put their best efforts into earning an honest living by doing the best job they can to help the organization they work for achieve its purpose. Whether that purpose is fighting terrorism, educating children, producing soap operas, or selling potato chips, there's really relatively little dysfunction out there. There are a lot of screwups, failures, and ineffectiveness, all of which are normal, fixable parts of life, but little dysfunction. That may not be what you hear and read about, but that's only because normal is boring, and no one gets paid to report on or dramatize normal.

So if you're just starting out in your career, don't feel you're entering a minefield or the career ward of a mental institution. Mostly, it's all good.

But it's not all good, which is why we need this chapter. Every career coach has clients with abusive or unfair bosses. Or clients who work for companies that won't succeed no matter how well their employees perform. Don't let the discussion get you down. Remember that these situations are called dysfunctional because they're not normal.

Read this chapter the way a pilot reads the chapters of his training manual that describe what to do if the engine of the plane he's flying suddenly quits. Nothing to worry about in the normal course of events, but if it happens and you're prepared, you can walk away unharmed. Don't be influenced by Dilbert's organization and his pointy-haired boss. In the real world, things aren't that bad at all. Your engine isn't going to fail on every flight.

BEST BOSSES

Let's say you work for a boss who's ineffective or even wholly incompetent. Maybe your boss is smart enough but her management style doesn't motivate people, or she's not good with customers, or she's simply guided by ill-conceived strategy or tactics. Maybe she's trying to minimize costs when she should be trying to maximize quality, or she's out to maximize market share when she should be trying to maximize profits instead. Or it could be that she simply doesn't have the knowledge, skills, qualities, or ability to do her job properly.

If you work for the public school system, maybe the school superintendent hasn't put into place a program for improving teacher effectiveness and student college acceptance rates. If you're in law enforcement, perhaps the department head is an ex-military type who isn't comfortable dealing with domestic abuse or sex crimes and has allowed these areas to become a blot on the department's record.

Whatever the reason or the situation, your boss is not producing the desired results, and you're stuck reporting to him. Let's go a step further and say the entire management team you work for is ineffective. It not only happens, but unlike real dysfunction, it's distressingly common in organizations. So what do you do if you're in the middle of this mess?

First off, you should be thankful for your good fortune. Everyone may be complaining about how incompetent your boss or the management team is, but all you should hear is opportunity knocking. Believe it or not, if you're out to achieve Outstanding Success, you're probably in the right place. If everything's screwed up because your boss and other managers are ineffective, you're in an opportunity-rich environment.

A really good sales manager, for example, always prefers taking over a territory where no one is making anywhere near quota rather than a territory where everyone is killing the numbers. He knows that good, competent sales management can result in outstanding improvements in the disaster territory, while delivering equivalent improvements in the already outstanding territory is almost impossible.

If you don't believe working for someone who is incompetent is the best thing that can happen for your career, consider the opposite example of Drew.

Drew was a senior manager in charge of systems development for a large, sophisticated financial services company. His annual budget exceeded $100 million, so we're talking about a very significant management responsibility.

It was Drew's misfortune that his boss knew as much about managing systems development as he did, because systems development was an area Drew's boss had managed, studied, and written about. Although Drew's job was exciting, intellectually challenging, and central to the company's success, Drew confided to me that the years he worked in that job were among the most stressful in his career. Although his boss was a perfectly reasonable manager whom Drew admired and got on well with, his boss's competence made him difficult to impress. Worse, because Drew's boss had the department functioning well even before Drew took over, there was little Drew could do that anyone would consider to be truly Outstanding Performance.

Although he succeeded in his job, he left after only two years to work for someone who had little understanding of computing technology. While Drew's old boss always saw him as doing a good job, his new managers quickly saw him not merely as doing a good job, but as an Outstanding Performer.

So stop complaining about how ineffective your boss or everyone around you is, and get to work making things better. When things are a mess, it's often a relatively straightforward matter for a logical, organized, and goal-oriented person to set things right and to make herself and the people around her into Outstanding Performers. It's much more difficult when the organization you join is already outstanding. Then you have to be outstanding squared before people see you as an Outstanding Performer.

This doesn't mean the organizations you work for have to be second-rate for you to have opportunities to excel. It often happens that the most exciting, most successful, and fastest-growing organizations are the most in need of competent and effective people. Everything is happening so fast, it's impossible to keep up, and there are messes and opportunities everywhere. So whether you target moribund organizations that need a shot in the arm or highly successful organizations growing too quickly to keep up with everything that has to be done, being surrounded by ineffectiveness and incompetence is not necessarily a bad thing.

But there is a big difference between ineffective or incompetent and dysfunctional. All bets are off if the person you work for or the entire organization is dysfunctional. For while ineffectiveness and incompetence are likely to increase your chances to deliver Outstanding Performance and achieve Outstanding Success, dysfunction may make it impossible. Because dysfunctions are so important to your ability to achieve Outstanding Success, it's important to understand and recognize their three forms—strategy, management, and behavior.

DYSFUNCTIONAL STRATEGY

The first form of dysfunction, dysfunctional strategy, occurs at the highest levels in an organization and influences everyone. Dysfunctional strategy happens when a boss or an entire management team is committed to a strategy that is likely to cause the organization distress or even to fail.

In business, a common example of this in publicly traded companies is when the company's senior management allows or even encourages an undue focus on short-term financial results that causes long-term damage. Sometimes senior managers engage in this short-term maximizing strategy in response to pressure from shareholders demanding short-turn stock appreciation. Sometimes, however, company executives do it to increase the value of their stock options or performance bonuses that are tied to short-term results.

An extreme example of dysfunctional strategy occurred in several companies headed by Al "Chainsaw" Dunlap. Dunlap's exploits are documented in the book *Chainsaw: The Notorious Career of Al Dunlap in the Era of Profit-at-Any-Price* by John A. Byrne. Dunlap and his management team drastically cut staff; closed plants; and reduced capital investment, research and development, and product development in an effort to make the companies they were running look as good as possible as quickly as possible. Their strategy was to improve the apparent performance of the company to sell it before the bottom fell out. This is a classic, if somewhat extreme, example of strategy dysfunction—a persistent pattern of short-term practices that makes the company weaker in the long term.

Interestingly, I was once involved with a strategically dysfunctional company that failed because its management followed practices almost directly opposite to Dunlap's. Instead of underinvesting in the long term, the company's management invested too much in the long term, and specifically, in product development.

The company's strategy was to be the technology leader and offer the technically most advanced and elegant product in the market. Pursuing this strategy, the management invested nearly all the company's limited resources in expanding and perfecting its product, to the point where little remained to spend on marketing and sales. The company failed because its product strategy wasn't supported with an effective selling strategy.

In the public sector, the decision by FEMA (the Federal Emergency Management Agency) to allow a focus on terrorism to dramatically reduce its interest in and ability to respond to natural disasters like hurricanes was a dysfunctional strategy. New Orleans paid the price.

What does all this high-level stuff have to do with you, someone toiling away deep in the company? As it turns out, plenty.

Whether you're a senior manager or the newest entry-level employee with no say in the organization's strategy, the organization is the platform for your career. Its strategy influences your chances of achieving Outstanding Success. If you were a manager in one of Al Dunlap's companies and trying to build a career, you would fail because the company's strategy was dysfunctional. Although Dunlap and a few people close to him earned small fortunes before he was found out and his career imploded, the likelihood that you or any other normal person would achieve Outstanding Success working anywhere in such a company is essentially zero.

Whether you're a key player or just a small cog in the organization's wheel, you must be careful about hitching your star to an organization guided by a dysfunctional strategy. You do not want to work somewhere that will fail and take you with it, even if you consistently deliver Outstanding Performance.

So how do you know if you're working for an organization following a dysfunctional strategy? First, let's not kid ourselves: it may not be possible to know. Many of the people who worked for Enron, for example, had no idea their company was a time bomb waiting to go off. Quite the contrary—they believed they were part of a new order, a company that was changing the world for the better. So people get fooled. It happens.

But not everyone was fooled. Many people were in positions where, if they paid attention to what was happening, they would have known there was rot in the foundation. There was just too much mismanagement, too many failed projects, too much money being lost, too many deals that didn't make business sense. Many people, even people not very high up in the company, could see trouble was brewing, if they chose not to ignore obvious signs. But most of those who saw or suspected that all was not right looked the other way because their earnings were high and their stock options and 401(k)s looked like winning lottery tickets. Too many rode the train to its disastrous end.

If your goal is to achieve Outstanding Success, it's your responsibility to thoroughly understand the organization you work for. You are not a medieval peasant toiling away in the countryside under the thumb of rulers who may be decrepit, self-serving, or dysfunctional. If you don't like the way management is running the show and it's not in your power to change things, and if you believe the strategic problems are permanent, you must beat a hasty retreat. Pay close attention, and study your organization, its managers, and its competitors. Sure, you may be fooled, but just as likely, if the organization is headed in the wrong direction, you'll begin to suspect something is wrong before you're with it for too long.

Auditors at Arthur Andersen looked the other way when certain large, profitable clients booked sales and expenses improperly. People in the firm had to know that their company was violating sacred accounting standards, but no one wanted to risk tightening things up and possibly losing clients generating millions in fees. When regulators finally exposed the shoddy practices, the venerable accounting firm of Arthur Andersen was no more. All its employees lost their jobs.

Mortgage brokers and their managers working in the subprime market segment saw lending standards drop to the point where the family gerbil could have qualified for a mortgage. Many mortgages turned out not to be legitimate, while legitimate homeowners defaulted on their loans when they found they couldn't make their payments, often without knowing what it was they had committed to. The results were entirely predictable, even if the timing wasn't. Thousands of people working in the mortgage industry who thought they were on their way to achieving Outstanding Success lost their jobs instead.

These are examples of companies with dysfunctional strategies whose employees at all levels suffered when the chickens came home to roost. Of course many were surprised and unprepared for the disasters their careers faced. But others simply ignored obvious signs of dysfunction. Their prevailing attitude was: "We're not the CEO, we have no say about strategy. And hey, the money's coming in, so go with the flow."

Don't be a passive employee who just does a job and takes home a paycheck. Study the organization you work for, and get to know the environment it works in, the people it serves, its competitors, the laws governing its operations, the standards people hold it to, and its strategies. It doesn't matter if you're the CEO or in your first job. If you keep your common-sense meter tuned to sensitive, you'll soon begin to feel uneasy if something is wrong. Sure, the job of setting strategy may be far from you, but as the old saying goes, If you lie down with dogs, you'll get up with fleas.

DYSFUNCTIONAL MANAGEMENT

In chapter 6, "Take Ownership," we talked about the need to treat the organization you work for as if you owned it. What that means, essentially, is to be sure your personal objectives are aligned with the organization's objectives. No one likes someone who's feathering his own nest at the expense of the people around him and the organization generally. When people realize what you're doing, you'll find your support eroding as you lose their trust and they question your every move.

Fine, but it has to work both ways. It's not enough for the organization to be following an effective strategy and be succeeding if that success is the result of management practices that don't allow *you* to succeed. Having the organization's success come at your expense is as bad as having your success come at the expense of the organization.

That was the case in a forty-person police department that served a suburb of a major city. The department is actually well managed and effective, in the sense that it uses its resources efficiently and has a high crime-close rate. But some of the best officers are passed over for promotion to sergeant or denied other career opportunities (detective sergeant, SWAT, firearms trainer) because the brass feels "they are too valuable at what they do." The more qualified, better-performing officers who can't pick up their families and leave for another law enforcement job elsewhere face years, even decades, of demoralizing stagnation in the same job.

While the organization and its three senior officers meet their goals, they do so at the cost of many of the best performers being unable to meet their own. The performance of the department notwithstanding, this is dysfunctional management if you're an outstanding performer looking to achieve Outstanding Success.

As another example, the armed services do not promote non-college-educated enlisted personnel to the officer ranks. This, for an outstanding enlisted person, is dysfunctional management. Bill Gates, Paul Allen, Michael Dell, Larry Ellison, and Kirk Kerkorian, none of whom graduated from college but all of whom became billion-aires (yes, that's with a *b*), wouldn't have advanced past the rank of sergeant had they chosen the armed services for a career.

If you work for an organization where no one gets ahead who hasn't graduated from an Ivy League school, or earned an MBA, or come up through sales, or isn't a white male Anglo-Saxon Protestant, or doesn't possess some other characteristic that has no bearing on performance, you're working for an organization that's suffering from dys-functional management. If you believe you can overcome this dysfunction and you love and are really good at what you do, stick with it. Otherwise, if your goal is to achieve Outstanding Success, you have to move on.

Greg was made a managing director of one of the country's major investment banks even though he worked in technology and no one in technology had ever been made a managing director in the company's sixty-eight-year history. Greg stayed with the firm because he believed that, despite its history, it was fundamentally a meritocracy whose senior managers would reward out-standing performance. He was right in his bet, and he wound up in a position with a seven-figure annual com-pensation.

But earlier he had left another firm because he be-lieved that performance, even Outstanding Performance, was far less valued than a path up the company's con-ventional career track. Only people who had been hired directly after receiving an MBA and who had progressed lockstep through a series of jobs in the company's vari-ous divisions and staff functions were ever considered for the highest senior management positions. Everyone else was just hired help, no matter how outstanding their performance might have been. Greg saw this as dysfunctional management that was unlikely to change, and he left a secure well-paying job for one where he felt it was at least possible to achieve Outstanding Success.

DYSFUNCTIONAL BEHAVIOR

It is an unfortunate fact of life that the world is full of people who, from the standpoint of the people they know and deal with regularly, behave dysfunctionally. Not to put too fine a point on it, these are life's jerks. Child and spouse abusers in families, bullies in schools, cheats and embezzlers in business, police officers or district attorneys who trample people's rights in order to win convictions, lawyers who knowingly exploit the law to line their own pockets. Some operate just over the line of legality, keeping their dysfunctional behavior barely within legal limits, but most are dysfunctional in perfectly legal ways.

From the standpoint of your career, dysfunctional behavior may take any of the following forms:

- **Bullies** are bosses and others in positions of responsibility who verbally abuse people or otherwise fail to show the proper respect owed to those who report to them or are lower in the organization's hierarchy.

- **Glory Hogs** take credit for the work, ideas, and accomplishments of others.

- **Ingrates** are people who don't appreciate those who work for them and don't acknowledge their efforts.

- **Control Freaks** don't give the people who work for them the freedom to become Outstanding Performers and achieve Outstanding Success.

- **Bigots** are prejudiced against people based on race, religion, gender, sexual orientation, where they attended school, or—well, or against anything that doesn't relate to performance.

- **Reprobates** are dishonest; they regularly lie, cheat, or steal.

- **The Threatened** are people who will not hire or promote people they feel are better, smarter, or more effective than they are for fear they will look bad, lose their position, or otherwise be at a competitive disadvantage.

This is a long list, and you may know of other dysfunctional behaviors to add to it. Often, the same person displays multiple dysfunctional behaviors. What all behavior dysfunctions have in common is that the people who exhibit them can prevent you from achieving Outstanding Success even if you deliver Outstanding Performance.

Stan works for a hundred-person retail company. His boss is, among other things, a Control Freak. For example, he controls every employee's access to e-mail, and he reads all e-mails before he gives his employees access to them. One employee received an e-mail from a family member informing him of a death in his family. The boss responded to the e-mail himself, passing along his condolences to someone he didn't know, before the employee to whom the e-mail was sent even had an opportunity to read the e-mail.

Stan's boss is also a Bully. He once sent an e-mail to Stan, saying simply, "I just want you to know that I know what you did, and I won't forget it." This might be funny if the boss had a sense of humor and was joking. But he didn't and he wasn't. In fact, Stan had done nothing and had no idea what his manager was referring to. The message was simply a bullying tactic the boss had used with other people in the company, but his behavior was so erratic that no one dared call him on it.

Of course this is outrageously dysfunctional behavior, but yet Stan has worked for this person for ten of the twelve years Stan has been with the company. Besides grousing with other employees, his only response is to look forward to the day his boss will retire or, if Stan is in any way normal, one day be hit by a bus.

Or consider Helen, who works for the Glory Hog boss who keeps the people who work for him hidden away. Whenever it's time to make a presentation to the company's management, whether to present the findings of a study his department has done or to get the annual budget approved, he always makes the presentation himself. Sometimes he takes along a single favorite, fawning assistant, but never the principal people who generated the work. They all joke that they know what it feels like to be kidnapped and locked in a basement room.

Then there's Rick, a Bully and Bigot of the first order who was a manager on the trading floor of a large investment bank. He screamed and cursed at people with abandon, personally attacking their intelligence, decisions, actions, and drive. He was especially disrespectful to women, treating the office like a singles bar where he could troll for extramarital sex. (He was eventually undone by a harassment suit.) He was an embarrassment to the company but tolerated because he was an effective and profitable trader.

How, you might wonder, can anyone tolerate working in such situations? How can such people continue to be employed by reasonable organizations? And finally, what can you do if you suddenly find yourself working for a person with such dysfunctional behavior?

Fortunately, we have other areas of life we can learn from. We can ask why a woman tolerates living with a partner who abuses her or the children. Or why people continue to live with an alcoholic. Or why parents continue to enable grown children to use drugs and fail in their lives.

In all cases, there are several factors at work. The first, and perhaps the most important, is that *people are treated by others as they allow themselves to be treated.* Abusers test their relationships, beginning with a single abusive act. If the abuser gets away with it, the abuse inevitably escalates. Unfortunately, too often the person on the receiving end tolerates the initial abuse because the consequences of confronting the abuser on what might be just slightly abusive behavior seem to be worse than just going along.

So the employee, worried about being fired or otherwise punished, just takes the abuse the first time he's called an idiot in front of others or she's inappropriately touched. The abuser's behavior is rewarded or, at the least, not punished, and the abuse continues, escalating ever so gradually over time.

If Stan's boss had intercepted his e-mail during his first day at work and responded to his family member without his knowledge, it's unlikely Stan would have let that pass. It would have been sparklingly clear that he was dealing with a seriously dysfunctional person. Whether Stan would have reported it to higher-ups, confronted his boss, or simply left the company isn't clear. But it's unlikely he would have tolerated it any more than a mother would tolerate a stranger walking into her home and abusing her children. Time and gradually growing dysfunction are usually needed for career people to become accustomed to accepting wildly dysfunctional behavior in work environments.

So what is the solution if you find yourself working for people who exhibit dysfunctional behavior? If you want it to stop, you must confront it immediately. No matter what the cost of dealing with the problem, the only certainty is that the problem will become much worse and the cost of dealing with it far greater. Stan, who works for the Control Freak and Bully, has nearly twelve years invested in the company he's working for. In his midfifties, he is now in a much less favorable position to leave and start over elsewhere than if he had confronted the problem initially and the worst happened and he had to find a new job.

Because no one confronted the trading floor manager, he continued to escalate his dysfunctional behavior for years. Things ended in a messy, publicly reported legal action that was finally brought by a woman who tired of his harassment. While she won the lawsuit in settlement shortly before it was to go to trial, she would have been far better off stopping the abuse at its start than suffering through the turmoil and career-destroying publicity of a lawsuit.

If you have the misfortune of running into dysfunctional behavior, the key is to recognize it and admit that you have been dealt a bad hand. Your only reasonable options are to throw in the towel and leave, or try to improve the situation by confronting the dysfunctional behavior before you're so far into the game that there's no hope of recovering completely. As primal as it may sound, an organization is a little like a playground from your childhood. Bullies and other abusers must be confronted. Going along is never a winning strategy.

Before leaving this topic, there is one final situation we should discuss. We've talked about the normal state of affairs in organizations being, well, normal, as most reasonable people understand that term. No one screams and shouts, no one bullies or takes credit for your work, there's little backstabbing, and people, to the best of their reasonable abilities, work toward the best interests of the organization. We've said that when things turn bad, they often do so in small steps, gradually increasing in dysfunction so that a new, decidedly nonnormal normal state exists.

But for some people it happens much more abruptly. These are people who are unlucky enough to begin their careers in dysfunctional situations. Never having been in healthy career situations, they don't know they're in careers they should escape from. It's like someone being raised in a dysfunctional family. They come to believe that the dysfunction they're experiencing is normal because that's all they've seen.

Know that if you have the misfortune of beginning your career in an environment that seems dysfunctional, it probably is. It may be a daunting task to confront people in a new organization or move on before you've settled down, but work should be fun. Above all, remember that you will be treated the way you allow people to treat you. You may not run the organization and you may be on the bottom of the totem pole, but you control how you allow other people to treat you. Don't take abuse of any sort, or you'll be doomed to take it forever.

CHAPTER 10

GETTING UNSTUCK

In this chapter:

How to get your career on track to achieving
Outstanding Success if you're stuck in an eddy.

*Men of age object too much, consult too long,
adventure too little, repent too soon, and seldom
drive business home to the full period, but content
themselves with a mediocrity of success.*

FRANCIS BACON

IT'S ALL YOU

The greatest gift fate can bestow upon you as a working man or woman is to love your work. I have known of a very few people fortunate enough to so love the work they do, they'd do it even if they weren't paid to do it: two judges who sat on the bench until they died, a musician who performed until he could physically perform no more, an NFL lineman, a few entrepreneurs who could never get out of the making-money game even though the last thing they needed was more money.

For most of us, if we won the $100 million Powerball lottery on Saturday, the last place you'd see us is at the office on Monday. But even if you wouldn't work if you didn't have to, it's still a great gift to love your work. So what if you take the gold watch or lottery check and head for the golf course or the beach house at the first opportunity? At least you had a good run and were happy throughout your career.

Unfortunately, two-thirds of all working people struggle through their working lives without loving their work. They search endlessly for career success and happiness without finding a direction, or drift through jobs and their career, or worse, end up as one of the Forlorn. What do you do if you're one of these people? You've made a wrong turn somewhere, and you're stuck in a job or career you no longer enjoy and that's not taking you where you thought your career would someday take you.

Very simply, you've got to set unstuck. How you manage your career when you're stuck is almost more important than how you manage your career when you're moving forward and all is going well. Like getting your car unstuck from a snowdrift, you have to go about it in a determined, logical way, and it will take more effort and energy to get unstuck than it would have taken to avoid getting stuck in the first place. But there you are with your career wheels spinning, and your only options are to stay bogged down for the next ten to thirty years or to somehow extricate yourself and start moving forward again.

The first step in getting your career unstuck is to take responsibility for being stuck. It's not your parents' fault because they didn't send you to the right schools or give you wise counsel when you were young. It's not your boss's fault because he's a jerk and is not giving you the opportunity to do your best. It's not your spouse's or children's fault because your family obligations prevent you from making changes or taking risks.

Your parents may have failed to guide you well, your boss may in fact be a jerk, and you may have important family obligations, but you're the master of your career. Besides, even if it's not entirely your fault that you're stuck (though it probably is), it's 100% your responsibility to get unstuck. If you cannot accept this simple truth, close the book, because you're going to spend the rest of your career stuck and nothing written here will help you.

Raj ran a small venture capital–backed technology company he sold just before the Internet bubble burst. His share of the proceeds was $20 million, but it was paid in the acquiring company's stock that couldn't be sold for a year following the transaction. Before Raj could cash out, the value of his stock dropped to $100,000. Ouch! He blamed the world for his misfortune—the acquiring company's management, his venture capital backers, the irrational exuberance of the Internet bubble.

While all or some of this may have been true, his company was never really worth what it was sold for, and he was the guy who agreed to sell the company for stock. But instead of accepting responsibility for his fate, he stayed stuck in a funk for years and destroyed his career by refusing to take any job that didn't guarantee him financial success.

Harold, on the other hand, felt his family obligations kept him from leaving his secure government job where he'd accumulated more than twenty years of pension benefits. If he hadn't been facing college expenses for three children and retirement in another twenty years, he was convinced he'd have taken a chance and moved on to more interesting and better-paying work in the private sector.

Sharon worked for Enron and lost both her middle management job and her 401(k) when the company crashed. She blamed Enron's management for her now being unable to find a job comparable to the one she lost. In point of fact, for years she was happy working in an overpaid support position that wasn't advancing her career. Instead of accepting responsibility for the difficult time she had finding a job and focusing on the future, she wasted time grousing with her old colleagues.

Sometimes bad things happen to good people, even people who thought they were making good decisions. If you're stuck, it's fine to think through what got you stuck, but now it's time to move on. If you're ready to accept responsibility for your own career destiny, let's begin the process of getting unstuck.

BREAKING OUT

Being stuck means you're not on a path to achieving Outstanding Success. If you want more from your career than it seems it will deliver, it's time to do something. But what? The answer depends on what phase you're in in your career.

Phase I—ages 18–24
Phase II—ages 25–34
Phase III—ages 35–54
Phase IV—ages 55–65

Let's look at each phase and the options available to you.

Phase I—Ages 18 to 24

It's not unusual for people in phase I of their careers to be in college with little idea of what they want to do when they graduate, or in entry-level jobs that they don't particularly enjoy and that are unlikely to lead to Outstanding Success. If that describes you, it's easy not to worry because there's a good chance you're comfortably among a group of friends who are in the same situation. But remember, very few of your friends will achieve Outstanding Success. Very few will even go through their careers truly enjoying their work. If you don't want to be part of this floundering group in ten or twenty years, this is the best time to do some serious career exploring.

Because you have accumulated little career experience, you forfeit little by abandoning a career path you tried but didn't like for a new direction. In that sense, you get a free ride during phase I; you can explore different career options at little cost to you. Also, employers understand that young people are still finding their place in life, so frequent job changes don't hurt you as they might later in your career.

What's perhaps most important during phase I is to understand you're not stuck in your job or, if you're still in college, in whatever subject area you're majoring in. If you're out in the world and working and you have car loan payments, rent, credit card debt, or other financial obligations that put you in a situation that limits your flexibility, shame on you. You can't let your next thirty or forty years be determined by the payments on a two-year-old Miata, a plasma TV, or even a mountain of student loans.

As perverse as it may sound given your lack of money as you're just starting out, money is just about the worst reason you can have for working during phase I of your career. Of course you want and need money as you're accumulating some of the basic necessities of life, maybe enjoying travel and freedom for the first time, perhaps even starting a family. And of course you should negotiate as high a compensation as you can. But working in a job doing something you love and are good at, one that makes it possible to deliver Outstanding Performance, is far more important than the money it pays during phase I.

Jill was a recruiter for one of the country's most exciting and fastest-growing technology companies, a company *Fortune* magazine identified as one of the best places in America to work. It was her first real job after college and a stint in the Peace Corps. Besides receiving outstanding salary and benefits, she was working in a stimulating environment with intelligent and motivated coworkers in a youth-oriented atmosphere closer to a college campus than a corporate organization.

But she was stuck in a job with low intellectual content that wasn't taking her in a direction she wanted to go. She was wasting valuable time doing work that didn't make her happy only because none of her other options paid so well or provided such attractive amenities.

The first things it takes to get unstuck in phase I are the insight that you're not progressing toward Outstanding Success and the courage to make the change no matter what the financial consequences. (Though the same is true if you're stuck in phases II, III, or IV.)

But what if you're in this first phase of your career and you can't seem to find a place in life where you're doing what you love to do and are good at, and that allows you to meet your objectives? Don't worry; keep trying. Like finding a life partner to love, finding a life's work to love can be very difficult or a matter of dumb luck. You must analyze yourself—your strengths, weaknesses, likes, and dislikes—and experiment until you've found work that not only pays the bills, but that suits you and will allow you to become an Outstanding Success.

Remember the story of Lynn in chapter 8? It took her five tries early in her career to find her passion—English to economics to political sciences to business, and finally to law. She was successful at everything she tried, but she refused to settle. The prospect for financial success alone wasn't enough. Being good at and loving what she did wasn't enough. She searched until she found what she was good at, loved doing, and that gave her the opportunity for financial success.

The most important thing you can accomplish during this first phase of your career is to find your Outstanding Success Zone—the work you love, are good at, and that will allow you to achieve your career objectives. Don't waste time during this early phase merely earning money in jobs that in the end do little but help you buy stuff you don't really need and can't really afford.

Phase II—Ages 25–34

The danger during phase II is that you may be stuck and not know it. Your earnings are growing; you're doing new stuff, so you're learning; and you're not unhappy. By this time you've been trained in something useful to the organization you work for—sales, production, planning, teaching, building systems, accounting, whatever. So you're really contributing, maybe getting positive feedback, being promoted, and you feel good about yourself. But if you're not working in your Outstanding Success Zone and you're not accumulating accomplishments through Outstanding Performance, you're just hired help the organization is paying to do things it needs done.

The good news is that it's relatively easy to make one of two kinds of changes during phase II. The first is to do what you're already doing but in a different organization—the classic job change. You do this if you like what you're doing and you're really good at it, but your current job doesn't put you in a position where it's possible for you to deliver Outstanding Performance. The nice thing about this type of change is that it usually comes with a promotion and/or compensation increase, but these are less important than moving into your Outstanding Success Zone and taking a job that allows you to deliver Outstanding Performance.

The second option is to do something different within the same organization, an option that's generally possible only if you've established a reputation as a high-potential person. A strategy for getting unstuck that's possible during phase I but that's almost never realistic during phase II is to change both what you do and the organization you work for at the same time.

Sam, at thirty-two years old, worked in IT at an investment bank and wanted to move to a job on the trading floor. He couldn't even get an interview at other financial services companies, much less a trading floor job. He was trying to change the company he worked for and what he did for a living at the same time. So he went to his boss and asked to be part of a group on the trading floor that worked with computers to build complex models for trading securities.

Although Sam had never worked on a trading floor, this was a reasonable request because the trading floor managers knew Sam, and he brought IT and analytical skills to the trading floor that they needed. Though his new job was not the trading floor job Sam really wanted, he was at least on the trading floor and intimately involved in its day-to-day functioning.

Once on the trading floor every day, Sam learned the business from the perspective of the front office and developed a reputation as an intelligent, hardworking analyst who brought real value to the job of developing quantitative trading strategies. Within three years he was permanently out of IT and a full-fledged member of the trading floor. Now Sam was in a position where he could move to another company if he so chose.

The bottom line is that being stuck during phase II, either as a Drifter or a Searcher, requires decisive action that may take courage, change, and risk. It's certainly not too late to make big changes, but even more than in phase I, time and career options are slipping by every day. Phase II is the last time it will be relatively easy for you to become unstuck. However difficult doing the right thing for your career may seem in phase II, it becomes much more difficult in phases III and IV.

Phase III—Ages 35-54

The people in the organization you work for, and this is people from the CEO down to administrative assistants in the know, have either consciously or subconsciously divided everyone in phase III into one of two groups:

• Players, those who will be given the chance to achieve Outstanding Success, and

• Supporters, those who will not.

For the Players, this is an exciting period. They receive ever bigger challenges, their compensation increases even more rapidly than during their early career years, and every job brings new learning and increased personal value. For Players, work isn't work—it's an adventure, a labor of love, the thing they most want to do and how they want to spend their time. These are the Heat-Seeking Missiles, and they can sense that they're approaching the heat source.

But for the Supporters, life takes a turn for the worse.

Sometimes it's a sudden, terrible turn, and sometimes it's the end of a gradual turn that has gone largely unnoticed or ignored for years. But there it is: work is no longer an exciting growth- and learning-filled adventure. The Supporters are stuck and in danger of joining the Forlorn.

If the organization sees you as a Supporter, breaking out in phase III will be difficult. You have two strategies: rapidly begin accumulating significant accomplishments through Outstanding Performance in the career you're in, or change careers and start over. If you stick with your current career, you've got to turn over a new leaf and stop just doing your job. You need to begin to hit home runs or you'll never break out. As we discussed in chapter 4, this means understanding what it is that's important to your organization and setting your own objectives so you deliver Outstanding Performance.

Unfortunately, if you're seen as a Supporter, you may have lost the chance to structure your job, set your own objectives, and deliver Outstanding Performance.

———————

Dick was a forty-five-year-old IT project leader who was ordinary in every respect. His projects were never great successes or failures, and executives he supported weren't particularly positive or negative about his capabilities and support. Then one day Dick found himself reporting to a thirty-five-year-old manager he'd hired as a systems analyst seven years previously. It was a wake-up call, and he resolved to do something to get his career back on track.

But he couldn't. Although the company was building new systems with exciting new technology, Dick's managers did not see him as a new technology thinker or a particularly effective project leader. Consequently, they assigned him to maintain the company's old technology systems, systems scheduled to be replaced gradually over the course of several years. Dick's only hope was to leave and join a company where he did not have a reputation that trapped him in a job where it wasn't possible to deliver Outstanding Performance.

Dick had worked for his company for more than twenty years and didn't want to leave, but he knew he'd be permanently stuck if he stayed. So he first learned the new technologies on his own by taking classes at a local community college. Still ignored by his company, he eventually landed a job with another company that gave him a chance to extricate himself from the career hole he'd dug for himself for twenty years.

Fear of being left permanently behind turned Dick into a Heat-Seeking Missile, and he succeeded in restarting his career. He was never going to be able to make up for the time he lost in the early phases of his career, but at least he was unstuck.

———

Perhaps the most important ingredient to successfully becoming unstuck in phase III of your career is the wake-up call that says in no uncertain terms that you're being left behind, you've wasted time and opportunities, and if you don't do something fast, you're going nowhere. Worse, you'll be unhappy for the rest of your career. The fix may involve risk, change, and uncertainty, but the alternative is far worse.

The second option for getting unstuck in phase III is to start over in a new career. Because this is the same option you will have in phase IV, we'll discuss this option as part of the phase IV strategies.

Phase IV—Ages 55-64

As the Players and Supporters of phase III enter the last phase of their career, the organization recategorizes them as:

• Winners,

• Topped-Outers, or

• The Endangered.

This phase IV sorting sometimes happens as a formal part of the organization's succession planning process, and sometimes it's just part of the organization's collective mind. But whether it happens overtly or not, if you're in the last ten to fifteen years of your career, people see you in one of these three groups.

Winners have already achieved Outstanding Success or are nearly there. They have important responsibilities and major compensation to match. Life is rarely dull for Winners, as they continually face new challenges. These are senior executives, university deans, law firm partners, school superintendents, top-ranked leaders of public agencies, the heads of research labs and hospitals. As they become older, they're in even greater demand.

Topped-Outers have established a place in their career but have risen as high as they will ever go. Their specific functional or operating expertise and experience is valuable, but only so valuable. Their security tends to be tied to a single organization, and unlike the Winners, their mobility decreases sharply as they become older.

While nowhere near the top 1% earners, Topped-Outers' compensation is relatively high and provides a comfortable living. They are vulnerable to losing their position at the table should turmoil occur in the top management ranks and cause the people who support them to leave, but for the most part they have staying power based on a network of supporters they've known for years.

Their children are grown and college expenses may be largely behind them, so they have a measure of financial comfort. While they are not progressing in their careers, they have a secure place and are accepted by their peers. They may not be moving up, but they remain employed until they retire. While this may not be what they foresaw in their youth, at this stage, for many it's good enough.

The Endangered are similar to the Topped-Outers in that they've reached as high as they will go in their careers, but they lack the reputation and support network of people that will provide them a measure of stability and security until retirement. Consequently, their compensation and position within the organization they work for are lower.

The Endangered are vulnerable to being replaced by younger people, because people know that compared to the Players coming up behind them, they have no upside potential. The Endangered are not only earning more money than they may be worth, but they are taking up intermediate positions needed for younger people on their way up.

In fairness, many of the Endangered are in this position because they have failed consistently to deliver demonstrable high value over their careers. They are the sales managers who sometimes meet their sales quotas and sometimes do not, IT professionals who rarely deliver on time and within budget or who have difficulty dealing with nontechnical users, teachers who teach the same subjects year in and year out and in no way distinguish themselves, financial people who have been faithful cogs in the wheels of many companies but have never contributed more than simply doing the jobs assigned to them.

If you're in phase IV and find yourself stuck as a Topped-Outer or as one of the Endangered, it is likely too late to follow the strategies set out in the previous chapters, at least not within the context of your current career. This is a cold, harsh judgment, but if you have not become an Outstanding Success by this point, people's perceptions of you will hold you back. You have three options:

· Retire early,

· Hang on, or

· Switch gears.

Let's look at each.

Early Retirement

The thing about achieving Outstanding Success is that it takes time—time to accumulate accomplishments, to make some mistakes and recover, to build a personal reputation that itself has value. By phase IV, you're not only running out of time, but as someone who isn't perceived as a Winner, you're starting from far behind. The fact is, if you can afford to retire early, it is often the best solution. Put down this book. Outstanding Success is no longer relevant. It's time to enjoy the rest of your life.

Hanging On

It can happen, of course, that you cannot afford to retire early, but you have no career options left that can realistically lead to achieving Outstanding Success. Or there is nothing outside of work that you're interested in doing if you retire.

Bill was a phase IV Topped-Outer who had been with the same company for twenty-five years. He was a company officer and earning good compensation, though he would never advance in his position or become a top 1% earner. His work, which was repetitive and predictable from year to year, was not particularly interesting.

He'd not come close to meeting the expectations he'd set for himself in his youth, but his life was not unpleasant. He did a job that needed to be done, he was treated with the respect accorded a senior officer in an important company, and working with longtime associates brought a degree of comfort and social pleasure. He was vulnerable should the company be acquired, a scare that resurfaced every few years, but otherwise his job was secure.

He enjoyed his children, grandchildren, and golf, but had no real passions or interests. Due to his age, compensation, and lackluster accomplishments, he was essentially unemployable outside his company. He knew he was stuck but gave little thought to becoming unstuck. He dutifully did his job, enjoyed the perks of his position, accepted that he was passed by and would report to people he began his career with or who were younger than he was. His plan was simply to ride it out until retirement or until something happened out of his control that caused him to lose his position.

If you are young and ambitious when you read this, you may choose to judge Bill harshly. Do not. For whatever reasons, he failed to achieve Outstanding Success and ran out of career options. He is taking the only reasonable option open to him—hanging on and making the best of it.

Starting Over

For the most part, this book is positive and optimistic, offering the prospect of extraordinary happiness and success to almost anyone who sets his or her mind to achieving Outstanding Success. All that's required is to manage your career according to the book's seven strategies.

It is easy to see, however, that readers might view these last several pages as far less positive and encouraging than the rest of this book. And in one sense they are, but only because they recognize the indisputable fact that life's options decrease with the passage of time. It may be a sad fact, but there's not much you can do that will lead to becoming the CEO of a Fortune 100 company by the time you retire at sixty-five if you're still managing accounts payable at fifty-five. So it would be disingenuous not to recognize that retiring early or hanging on are sometimes the only options open to many people.

There is, on the other hand, one option that is always available to nearly everyone, no matter what their previous experience or age—starting over. It may seem radical, risky, and even foolhardy to some, but many men and women do it, and many do it successfully. Fortunately, the strategies for succeeding if you start over are the same seven strategies we've talked about in this book. All that's different is people's perspective and expectations.

I recall a television commercial in which a middle-aged man lost his management job and became unstuck by opening his own business—a kite store. He was, seemingly for the first time in his career, happy with his work. He viewed having been laid off as a positive because it forced him to take an action he would not have taken otherwise.

While the commercial's story was likely made for TV, it in fact depicts the real-life experience of many phase III and IV professional and management people who are unhappy or unsuccessful early in their careers. Or they are people who, for one reason or another, have lost attractive career options.

Many professional women, for example, find that they have lost many of their career options by leaving their careers during their children's childhood years. So instead of trying to push against heavy resistance in the corporate world, they start their own businesses. Other people stuck in phase IV, seeing that they are doomed to remain in jobs they don't enjoy and that are unlikely to bring them happiness, chuck it all and buy a franchise business, open a bed-and-breakfast, or otherwise go into business for themselves, often in a field entirely removed from their first career path.

Switching gears and starting over is often the only career option for people in phase IV who have become stuck. And that route can work out far better than most people imagine. Early in my career, I was fortunate to have known and worked with Currier Holman, who started a new career in his fifties and cofounded Iowa Beef Processors. The company rapidly grew to become a very successful, very profitable Fortune 200 company under his leadership. He became an Outstanding Success during phase IV of his career by starting over.

It's possible to change careers even in phase IV and become an Outstanding Success, even the CEO of a major publicly traded company, but we must be realistic. Currier Holman and other unusual cases aside, few people who are not already senior managers of large organizations by age fifty-five become senior managers of large organizations.

We will talk at length about starting a business or buying a franchise in chapter 11, but the fact is that it is extraordinarily difficult to achieve Outstanding Success by starting your own business. Moreover, achieving Outstanding Success through your own business takes two things phase III and IV people don't have much of—time and money they can afford to lose. Those entering entrepreneurship for the first time late in life without a financial cushion to weather slow start-up periods, mistakes, and normal learning can find themselves facing financial ruin.

Nevertheless, people stuck in phase III or IV generally approach starting a business with somewhat different objectives than they would have had earlier in their careers. They are often far more troubled by not being happy with their work than with not having become top 1% earners. Money is not as important as it once was. It's time to do something that, even if it cannot conceivably result in making you a top 1% earner, will make you happy. Enter the kite store.

While this route may not lead to Outstanding Success as we've defined it, having a job you enjoy that will pay an income stream for as long as you wish to work is a valuable asset indeed. So the guy running the kite store may earn a fraction of what he earned as a middle manager for some mega-organization, but for the first time in decades he looks forward to the beginning of the work week. It may not be Outstanding Success, but it beats hanging on or, for some people, retirement.

SUMMING UP GETTING UNSTUCK

The good news for people stuck in their careers is that it's not all bad news. Of course the best strategy is to be a Heat-Seeking Missile and manage your career so you're never in a position where you have to think about becoming unstuck. But if you find yourself stuck in a career track or job that won't lead to achieving Outstanding Success while you're in phase I or II of your career, it's likely that some careful thought and decisive action will get you unstuck.

The downside is that whatever action you take may involve significant change, uncertainty, and risk. But the alternative of staying the course will almost certainly lead to mediocrity and a work life that lacks passion and meaning at best, and decades of unhappiness at worst.

The best strategy for most phase III people to become unstuck is for them to quickly and assertively execute on the seven career strategies of chapters 1 through 7. If they have waited too long and this is no longer a realistic route to Outstanding Success, a career change may be the only alternative. By phase IV, the alternatives narrow still further, as it is likely too late for this book's career management strategies. The strategies are now retiring early, hanging on, or starting over in a new career direction.

Of course some people achieve Outstanding Success starting late in life, and many more find happiness, even if they do not become top 1% earners. But this must come from a dramatically reduced set of alternatives. The key is to assess the alternatives realistically, whether a job or career change, starting a new business, or investing in a franchise business, and to take decisive action as soon as possible. The best time to become happy is as soon as possible, and you will never have more life options than you have today.

This chapter raised the prospect of starting your own business as a career option. It is a dream shared by many people working in progressive economies. But one characteristic shared by everyone who has never been an entrepreneur is an unrealistically rosy picture of the entrepreneurial life. This failure to understand the perils and harsh demands of being an entrepreneur has proved to be the downfall of the unwary.

The purpose of chapter 11 is to strip the emotion and wishful thinking away from the options of starting your own business, purchasing a franchise business, running a venture capital–backed business, or working for someone else's company. Which of these you choose will affect your career and your life for decades, so it's important to know the good, the bad, and the ugly before you make your decision and not after you learn through bad experience.

CHAPTER 11

THE
ENTREPRENEURIAL
OPTION

In this chapter:

- A realistic look at becoming an entrepreneur, raising venture capital, buying a franchise, or keeping the day job;

- What it takes to succeed as an entrepreneur; and

- Why keeping the day job is an underrated career option.

*Most people have no business
ever working for themselves.*

THOMAS J. STANLEY

RUNNING AWAY FROM SOMETHING,
NOT RUNNING TO SOMETHING

If there is a single fantasy shared by more people who work in the Corporate World than any other, it is not to become their company's president, not to be featured on the cover of *Fortune* or *BusinessWeek*, not even to make millions. It's to own their own business. Like people condemned to prison, millions working in the Corporate World secretly desire not to prosper where they are, but to escape.

Perhaps dreaming of working for yourself is understandable if we look at the way many who work in the Corporate World live. First, there's the daily commute, which people list as the single thing they hate more than any other. One of the primary reasons, and perhaps one of the worst reasons, that people want to start their own business is so they can work close to home and have a shorter commute.

Then there's the money, or more accurately, the lack of enough of it. Most Corporate World employees depend on a fixed number of paychecks a year to make the mortgage and car payments, provide for their children, pay the bills, and create a decent standard of living for their families. Unfortunately, for most people these paychecks don't increase fast enough to pay the monthly bills, much less have enough left over for weathering financial storms, paying for their children's future college expenses, and funding a comfortable and dignified retirement. If this is where decades of working for the Corporate World has gotten them, it's only natural for people to dream of starting their own business and, they naively think, keeping all the money their business makes for themselves and their families.

Finally, issues of personal control loom as large as financial ones. People working for companies owned by others usually feel they aren't masters of their own destinies. It's true whether you're at the bottom of the Corporate World or at the top. As an insightful CEO once told me, "As you rise higher in the company, you just get to be tyrannized by a better class of people."

So Corporate World people look wistfully at Bill Gates; Michael Dell; the founders of Yahoo!, Google, and YouTube; and the guy down the block who owns a successful restaurant, insurance agency, or chain of dry cleaning stores, and think, "That's what I should be doing." But more often than not, what they're really thinking of is running away from something, not running to something. And that's a dangerous way to make career decisions.

ENTREPRENEURIAL BLASPHEMY

Many red-blooded Americans, and especially those who fancy themselves entrepreneurs, venture capitalists, or other captains of industry, are going to be outraged at what I'm going to say next, so let me give this some perspective first.

My father was a classic entrepreneur. Businesses he started included new and used car dealerships, boat manufacturing, an insurance agency, an accounting service for small businesses, a mortgage company, a company that mass-produced mosaic tile art for furniture, a mobile home park, and a dance hall. Some of his businesses were successful and some failed. I lived through every one of these businesses and remember them well.

Most people consider me to be an entrepreneur. I've started three businesses, one of which I grew to sales of more than $115 million and took public. I was named Entrepreneur of the Year in North Carolina for Emerging Growth Companies, based on my work with that company. I actually have a plaque with my name on it that proclaims me to be an entrepreneur. Woo-hoo.

In addition to starting three companies from scratch, I was the CEO of two venture capital—backed businesses I took over from the original founders. In both cases the investors brought me in to try to save sinking ships.

Even with all this experience with business start-ups, I've still spent more than half my career as an employee of companies I didn't own or run. These companies included small to very large manufacturing companies to Wall Street financial institutions. I've held jobs as ordinary as grocery store checker earning $1 an hour to being the third-ranking officer and member of the board of directors of a Fortune 150 company with ten thousand people reporting to me. I was a managing director of one of the world's premier investment banks.

With that perspective, which I believe is balanced and accounts for the realities of both working for yourself and working for someone else, and of working for large companies, small companies, and start-ups, here is my advice regarding the advisability of starting your own business: DON'T EVEN THINK ABOUT IT! TURN AROUND AND RUN AWAY!

We've all heard stories about entrepreneurs who started businesses in their garages with $500, or who borrowed from their families, or who mortgaged their homes and went on to build billion-dollar businesses. And of course it happens. This is the stuff of entrepreneurial legend that attracts people to start their own businesses. But it also puts way too high a gloss on what is in fact a very tough way to make a living.

The average net income for a sole proprietorship in the United States is less than $7,000. That's per year, not per week or even per month. In any given year, 25% of those businesses that haven't already failed don't make any profit whatsoever.

The sad fact is that most people who invest in a new business lose all their investment, whether it came from their bank account, their relatives, or a second mortgage. On average, new businesses last only four years, with many having to declare bankruptcy, leaving their owners in financial ruin. (Between 13% to 18% of all personal bankruptcies are the result of a business failure.)

Of course working in the Corporate World also has its downsides. You can be laid off or fired, and it can happen even if you're an effective, productive employee. Fine, but compared to starting your own business, the risk of being fired or laid off, which on average is 2.5%, is far, far less than the risk of failing in a new business.

THE ENTREPRENEURIAL IMPERATIVE

There are people who will ignore my advice against becoming an entrepreneur because owning their own business and not working for anyone else is part of their DNA. Or they may be people without the background, experience, or education the Corporate World is looking for; or older people the Corporate World overlooks; or people who have somehow screwed up and no longer have good options in the Corporate World. These people don't really have any option except to start their own business, and they're right to ignore my advice.

Starting your own business is a very difficult way to achieve Outstanding Success, and *the greatest single asset an entrepreneur can have is not to have any other options*. For people without options, becoming an entrepreneur is not a choice to be struggled with, not a direction to abandon in the face of hardship and challenge. It's an imperative.

So how do you know if you're one of the very few people who should start their own business? Very simple. If you have to think for more than five minutes about whether you should work for a company or start your own business, you shouldn't start your own business. If you feel you don't have any reasonable place in the Corporate World, or if every molecule in your being demands that you work for yourself, then you don't really have any decision to make, and you're one of the few who should start their own business.

THE SUCCESSFUL ENTREPRENEUR

This is a book about career management and not a book on entrepreneurship. But the dream of becoming an entrepreneur, of working for oneself, of going it alone, of becoming the next Bill Gates, has such an influence on people and the way they think of their careers that we need to consider the entrepreneurial career option in some depth. Specifically, let's look at the following six characteristics people need to succeed as entrepreneurs:

- An entrepreneurial vision

- Timing

- An entrepreneurial mind-set

- The ability to sell

- The ability to execute

- Luck

This is more than most people imagine, and much of it is, unfortunately, out of the entrepreneur's control. Let's look at each in turn.

An Entrepreneurial Vision

An entrepreneurial vision is simply a product or service idea that you believe people will pay money for and that you can provide at a profit. This can be as brilliant as the latest product or service that medical or information technology can provide, or as practical as thirty-minute pizza delivery. Moreover, this doesn't even have to be an original vision.

A product called VisiCalc was the original spreadsheet software product. (If VisiCalc wasn't the first spreadsheet, I apologize to the original genius, whomever that may be, behind this culture-changing idea. VisiCalc was the first to gain widespread market traction.) Its developers were true visionaries, able to see how emerging personal computer technology could be put to wide use by hundreds of thousands of people. VisiCalc was sold to Lotus Development Corporation, where it was developed into Lotus 1–2–3. The founder of Lotus did not have to envision a business built around a spreadsheet product; that vision already existed. His vision was a spreadsheet product that worked better and was easier to use than VisiCalc.

Then Microsoft came along with Excel, yet another spreadsheet product. Its vision was for a spreadsheet that integrated tightly with the personal computer's operating system and with other office applications.

Similarly, there may already be a dozen Italian restaurants, insurance agents, or landscape architects in your town. You don't have to invent a new product or service to become a successful entrepreneur. But you have to have a vision for where your business fits in, for why people will pay you enough money for whatever you do so you can earn a return on your investment, pay yourself for your time, and hopefully, earn a profit as well. Contrary to what many people think, this doesn't necessarily take business genius, but it does take common sense and an understanding of the marketplace you're going to be selling to.

Unfortunately, the entrepreneurial vision many people have when they start their new business is wrong, meaning that it will not support an actual business. They become transfixed with an idea that, over the kitchen table, in the bar, or even in the offices of the venture capitalists who are going to fund it, seems to be a can't-lose moneymaker that the world needs badly. So the investors invest, the entrepreneur establishes the business, and the bets are on the table. Then reality, competition, changing technology, and all manner of unpredictable factors show the entrepreneurial vision for what it really is—a bad idea that will not support the investors and the entrepreneur, much less generate a profit. This outcome is the rule, not the exception.

Glenn developed a new approach for developing computer-based business systems that he and his small team were able to prove in controlled tests greatly increased the productivity of systems development staff. The approach could save companies that adopted it millions in IT expenses and greatly improve the support their IT functions provided to the companies they were a part of.

This was not just another unsubstantiated marketing claim. The computer science department of one of the country's leading universities proved the results in published studies over a four-year period. Moreover, the approach was easier to learn and use than conventional approaches to developing systems. It was a proven, sure-fire product selling into a marketplace crying out for improved productivity. It couldn't lose.

Except it did. Although the new venture executed well and got off to an encouraging beginning, competition flooded the market with competing products, hidebound IT departments were reluctant to leave approaches they'd been brought up with, and conservative company managements stepped back from buying such an important product from a small start-up company. In the end, what seemed to all to be a brilliant product vision struggled to survive in the real-world markets.

Timing

Nothing will so quickly destroy a good idea, even a great idea, along with the visionaries behind the idea, as bad timing. As of this writing, the social networking Web site MySpace is a blockbuster success. Yet its entrepreneurial vision of a Web site where friends could gather electronically, meet others, and share personal stories was anything but new or unique when MySpace was founded in 2003. Years earlier, sites such as Six Degrees and SocialNet failed because they came to market before the market was ready to accept the idea. Timing may not be everything if the timing is right, but timing is everything when the timing is wrong.

Another high-tech entrepreneur came to market with a software tool built to increase the productivity of C++, then the most popular object-oriented programming language in the United States. But within six months the Java language began to rapidly overtake C++ within the object-oriented programming community. The entrepreneur's product became impossible to sell to a market that was anticipating an eventual wholesale move to Java, the next new thing. In this case, bad timing came in the form of a new technology that made the entrepreneur's product obsolete.

In both these situations, as in so many other entrepreneurial endeavors, it was difficult to fault the entrepreneur's vision. It's unrealistic to expect founders to predict the timing of unpredictable disruptive events that will topple their product or when a market is finally ready to embrace a new direction. Visionaries have their visions when inspiration strikes, and that may not at all be when the market is ready to embrace the vision. Which is one reason Leonardo da Vinci is better known as a painter than as an aeronautical engineer, despite his prescient plans for a helicopter.

An Entrepreneurial Mind-set

For entrepreneurs, catastrophe often has a hair trigger, and entrepreneurs need an entrepreneurial mind-set to avoid the failures in judgment that can set it off. An entrepreneurial mind-set is characterized by uncommon common sense, unwavering persistence, and a niggardly approach to spending money.

There is no test for when these three characteristics meet the minimum requirements for entrepreneurship, but there should be, because unlike Corporate World managers, entrepreneurs often perform without a safety net and with no room for error. A bad hire, a foolish purchase, a failed product launch that would cause no more career damage than perhaps a mention in an annual performance appraisal in the Corporate World, can lead directly to end-of-game for the entrepreneur.

Of course it's possible to learn the entrepreneurial mind-set, and many people do. But if you're not the child of an entrepreneur or you have not been raised in circumstances of want and constant danger of financial peril, have never worked for an entrepreneur, or have not learned how to be an effective entrepreneur the hard way—by trial and error—expect that your first entrepreneurial effort will fail. As perhaps will your second, third, and fourth.

If you have been a successful manager in a successful company, double the probability you will fail as an entrepreneur. It's not that some of what you learned as a manager may not be useful to you as an entrepreneur, especially if what you learned working for a big company is how to sell, but big-company habits are absolutely deadly when you're on your own.

James, the son of a college history professor, worked as a senior manager of a large technology company for twenty years before setting out on his own. Well, on his own and with the help of more than $40 million in venture capital. He used the money to lease costly office space fully three times larger than the company could conceivably use during the lease term, hire administrative and technical staff at top salaries, and assemble a full sales and marketing team long before the product was ready for sale.

The company ran out of money before it could produce a salable product. James was extraordinarily successful working as a manager for a large company but had exactly the wrong mind-set for an entrepreneur.

The Ability to Sell

The only thing the average person hates worse than being sold to is having to sell. For most people who don't sell for a living, selling seems manipulative, dishonest, maybe even degrading. In their hearts they believe that if what they have to offer is worthy, it should be enough to describe it honestly and buyers will line up. And perhaps it should work that way, but it doesn't. In my book *Three Steps to Yes: The Gentle Art of Getting Your Way*, I emphasize that "Unfortunately, the people in your life won't necessarily do what you want just because you happen to be right. They need to be persuaded."

This holds double if you're an entrepreneur. In the end, every entrepreneur has to sell—a lot. They have to sell to investors, employees, customers, suppliers, board members, landlords, recruiters, the press, to everyone. If you can't sell or you won't lower yourself to be constantly selling, selling, selling, don't even think about becoming an entrepreneur.

During the Internet boom in the late 1990s, I was hired as a consultant by an entrepreneur to help his new company develop its business plan. He assembled his management team for a three-day off-site meeting I was to lead. When I walked into the room, there were fourteen bright-eyed managers looking up at me, enough to run a $100 million business, even though the business had sales of less than $5 million. My immediate reaction was, "Uh-oh!"

But things got worse, much worse, as I was introduced to the managers and told their responsibilities. Every conceivable corporate function was covered except one—no one was in charge of sales! Worse, no one saw this as a problem or in any way unusual. Times were good, Internet businesses were booming, and everyone in the company, including the founder, considered classical selling to be so "old economy." Predictably, the business failed as soon as the new economy turned out to be not that different from the old economy and business stopped walking in the door.

The Ability to Execute

It is likely that more brilliant entrepreneurial visions have died of the disease of poor execution than any other cause. Poor execution opens the way for lesser competitors, drives even the most enthusiastic customers away, and frustrates good employees who abandon poorly run companies for ones providing greater job satisfaction.

Friendster is a social networking site that did almost everything right. It was not the first in the market, but its timing was perfect. It quickly grew to be the market leader, attracting a wide following of users and an all-star cast of investors and top-notch employees. But it failed to execute.

A 2006 *New York Times* article reported, "As Friendster became more popular, its overwhelmed Web site became slower. Things would become so bad that a Friendster Web page took as long as 40 seconds to download. . . . technical difficulties proved too pedestrian for a board of this pedigree. The performance problems would come up, but the board devoted most of its time to talking about potential competitors and new features. . . ." At the time the article appeared, Friendster had squandered its lead through poor execution and ranked fourteenth among social networking sites, coming in even behind myYear-book.com, a year-old site started by a sixteen-year-old high school student.

Sadly, this is not an unusual story. Have a bad meal at an independent restaurant, and you're experiencing poor execution on the part of the entrepreneur. Bad customer service or discourteous employees at a local store—poor execution on the part of the entrepreneur. Dirty rest-room—poor execution. Everything in the business is wonderful but it's not making money—poor execution. For any specific business, there are a hundred ways the entrepreneur can execute so poorly that he goes bust, and relatively few ways he can execute well and succeed. Executing well requires an intimate understanding of the product and the customers and a fanatic attention to every detail of operating the business, delivering the product or service, and taking care of the customer. Unfortunately, too many entrepreneurs fall woefully short.

Luck

Finally we come to what may be the most important factor in entrepreneurial success—luck. We said in the introduction that luck is what happens to you after you've set the game, after you've established the probabilities of winning and losing. You play a large part in how lucky you are or aren't, but at some point chance takes over. As it turns out, chance plays a far bigger role in the lives of entrepreneurs than it does for most people, because businesses often fail due to actions of competitors or the emergence of new technologies that are difficult for the entrepreneur to predict and adjust to.

Many entrepreneurs offered personal computer hardware during the early years of the personal computer's introduction. It was a catfight for the attention of consumers and business users and for distribution channels. Then IBM entered the fray and set a worldwide standard for personal computer architecture, an action the early personal computer entrepreneurs couldn't control and which sounded the death knell for most of the early personal computer providers.

This phenomenon is hardly limited to high technology. Have a Wal-Mart or Home Depot move into town, and dozens of small and medium-size well-run stores will fail, bankrupting their entrepreneur owners.

Perversely, in a free market system, it is sometimes the entrepreneur's success that can lead to her downfall. If the entrepreneur's vision is not protected by patents or copyrights, and few are, success breeds new competitors and imitators and attracts the attention of large, well-established, and well-funded competitors. Overnight a business can go from high growth and profitability to circling the drain.

Many people believe the MP3 player was an Apple innovation, but it was not. There were MP3 players long before the iPod, and their success attracted Apple. The company put its considerable design talents behind the concept and introduced its own product, together with a site for downloading music. Apple's products quickly came to dominate the market and suffocate the other offerings.

Perhaps an argument can be made that any of these MP3 companies could have developed as good a product as the iPod, but that argument ignores the realities of free markets. Well-financed followers into a market can learn from the mistakes of the leading entrepreneurs and the reactions of the buyers, and can fund product development and research that small companies can't afford. Established companies or the second or third wave of entrepreneurs have a decided competitive advantage when they enter a market after the first entrepreneurial visionaries have spent their development capital and exposed their crude first and second versions of their products to the harsh light and criticism of the marketplace.

I had, at this point, originally intended to say that none of this discussion was meant to discourage people from becoming entrepreneurs, that entrepreneurship was what made this country great, blah, blah, blah. Then I realized I wasn't being completely honest. My intent is in fact to discourage people who have no business becoming entrepreneurs from starting their own businesses.

Furthermore, it is an oversimplification to say that entrepreneurs are what made this country great. Sure, they contributed, but so did big business. It may have taken an entrepreneur to start IBM, Disney, Intel, Apple, Wal-Mart, and Google, but it took the people who run big businesses to make them the worldwide icons and wealth generators they have become.

But entrepreneurship has become so glorified in Western culture (and increasingly in modern Asian cultures) that people worship it without understanding precisely what it is they're worshiping. The press and public have exaggerated the virtues of entrepreneurship while at the same time exaggerating the melancholy and depression of working in the Corporate World. This chapter provides balance. And for balance, we also need to better understand life in the Corporate World. But first, let's consider two variations on true entrepreneurship and life in the Corporate World—starting a company using venture capital or buying a franchise. In terms of both risks and rewards, both are in between true entrepreneurship and becoming a full-fledged member of the Corporate World.

THE DRIVE-BY ENTREPRENEUR

There is now a relatively new phenomenon in the Western business world—"entrepreneurs" who start businesses using other people's money. With no disrespect intended (I've done it myself, three times), I call these people drive-by entrepreneurs.

Drive-by entrepreneurs may invest some small amount of their own money as seed capital before professional investors come in with the real risk capital, and they may participate in a small way with the professional investors in the ongoing financing of the new business. But the true financial risk is borne by professional investors (who are themselves usually investing other people's money), not by the company's founders.

The founders work for the company as employees and collect paychecks just like every other employee. They receive stock options they can cash in if the company is successful, but by the time the company is successful enough to sell or take public, the founders' ownership is typically a small percentage, having been diluted through multiple financing rounds. Still, the upside potential is there.

If the company tanks, the founders don't lose their homes or declare bankruptcy, as would classic own—100%-of-the-stock-and-take—100%-of-the-risk entrepreneurs. Failed drive-by entrepreneurs start another company funded by different investors or go to work in the Corporate World.

None of this is meant to take away from all the creative people, typically young people, who have good ideas and can persuade investors, typically old people, to invest in them. The drive-by entrepreneurial route is a viable option to achieving Outstanding Success, and has both advantages and disadvantages compared to becoming a true risk-taking entrepreneur or to taking a conventional job in an existing company.

But I have been an entrepreneur and a drive-by entrepreneur, and I have worked in the Corporate World, and I can state unequivocally that being a drive-by entrepreneur has far more in common with working in the Corporate World than it has with being a true entrepreneur. Being a drive-by entrepreneur is to true entrepreneurship what playing paintball is to being a marine stationed in Iraq.

While it's true that both classic entrepreneurs and drive-by entrepreneurs are people with creative business ideas who start businesses, it's the entrepreneurs who take all the financial risk and who operate without the safety net of a guaranteed paycheck. In reality, drive-by entrepreneurs are employees working for the investors. Nothing attests to this as much as the fact that venture capitalists fire or replace most founders with professional managers as soon as the company begins to show signs of success and growth. Venture capitalists shop for new CEOs the way owls hunt for field mice.

So let's keep the entrepreneurial currency pure and group the drive-by entrepreneurs with the Corporate World employees who don't have to risk their personal assets to start and run a business. If you have a good idea and can get someone to fund it, go for it. Unless you are absolutely driven to own a controlling interest in your company, that is usually a far better alternative than maxing out your credit cards and taking out a second mortgage on your home, to say nothing of persuading your in-laws to take out a second mortgage on their home and lending you the money.

And if you think you have a good idea but you can't get anyone to fund it, take this as a message. Either you don't really have a good idea or you don't have the selling ability that's required to succeed in your own business.

BUYING A FRANCHISE

We've said that an entrepreneur needs an entrepreneurial vision and mind-set, timing, the ability to sell and execute, and luck to become successful. Frankly that's a lot to ask of your average above-average person. Which is where franchising comes in. It's a way to get some of the wonders of entrepreneurship without all of the reckoning. Maybe.

But maybe it isn't. So before beginning this discussion

on franchises, it's important to warn readers that franchising has been rife with frauds, cheats, and charlatans who have duped many people out of some or all of their life's savings and some or all of their spirit. The situation was so bad that lawmakers put in place an impressive body of franchising law in an effort to protect aspiring, naive franchisees.

While good laws unquestionably offer a measure of protection by flummoxing crooks too stupid to figure out how to break the laws without getting caught, they are hardly a guarantee that the franchise you're considering will deliver what you expect. Competent and clever predators, wolves in sheep's clothing who mingle among the legitimate sheep, manage to find their way through legal obstacles to get at their prey. So be especially wary if you're considering buying into a franchise.

But with that warning, it's also true that many people have become happy, wealthy, and independent—or at least one or two of these three—through franchise ownership. The great value of a good franchise is that it drastically reduces the need for good timing, entrepreneurial vision and mind-set, luck, and the ability to sell and execute. People who buy a McDonald's franchise, for example, buy the McDonald's entrepreneurial vision, a ready McDonald's hamburger market others have figured out how to sell to, a proven formula for store location, a preselected list of proven restaurant equipment, and extensive training on how to execute well, right down to how much salt to add to the French fries, and at what time to stop serving Egg McMuffins.

All good franchises result in dramatically lower risk compared with a clean-sheet entrepreneurial start-up.

Invariably, however, they also come with lower upside potential. There is only so much profit potential in any given business opportunity, and experienced franchisers work to keep as much as possible for themselves while still keeping the franchisee working in the franchiser's system.

The end result is often that a franchise owner is more a captive manager than a true entrepreneur, though admittedly, a manager with a personal financial stake. Netted out, many franchisees are "buying a job" in the form of a formula business when they purchase a franchise.

I once examined a retail franchise opportunity for a friend that had a cost of roughly $1 million. This was a well-established and successful chain of retail stores servicing a segment of a crafts and hobby market. After a thorough analysis of the projected operating statements and talks with franchisees, we projected that the store would return $125,000 per year to my friend, though always with the risk that competition from big-box stores, catalog operations, and Internet suppliers could reduce this return or even turn it to a loss.

But assuming that all went as planned, $125,000 annual return was barely sufficient to provide both a return on capital invested and compensation for the owner's time. Assuming a 7.5% return on capital invested ($75,000)—not a high return given the risk associated with the investment—the owner would receive $50,000 for running the store, a very modest amount given the store's complexity, energy demands, and risk.

The bottom line is that had my friend decided to buy the franchise; for his $1 million investment he would be buying a 7.5% return on capital invested and a $50,000 job. (This ignores the possibility that the store might increase in value over time and provide an additional return when sold, but we viewed that as unlikely for reasons not important to detail here.)

The only difference between this opportunity and many other franchises is that this one did provide a return on capital as well as a job. Often, all a franchise investment buys the franchisee is a job. But it's a job that has you working for yourself. For many people that's an investment well worth the money.

THE CORPORATE WORLD

We've looked at the career options of becoming an entrepreneur, a drive-by entrepreneur, and a franchisee. Not only are they not for everyone, they're not for most people. Does this mean that the rest of us are doomed to a life of stultifying commutes, limited opportunities, intellectual boredom, and crushing dependency working for others? Far from it.

Working for a corporation today is really an amazing concept unparalleled in history. For most of its more than two million years on earth, humankind has had to use 90% of its energy just finding enough to eat. Things were hardly better during the early stages of organized business, right up through the industrial revolution. Corporations became the dominant employers and the most important force in commerce, and they held the balance of power over workers. (Although partnerships, limited liability partnerships, and professional partnerships are not strictly corporations, I include them in this discussion under the term "corporations.")

It was a power they often abused. Through most of the history of organized business there were no foosball

tables in employee lounges, 360-degree performance reviews, and off-site employee training in Orlando. Think
instead of real-life Bob Cratchits slaving away in offices
and Oliver Twists exploited by factory owners.

But as companies became even larger and more powerful, they gradually absorbed the bulk of the workforce,
bringing supply and demand more into balance. Especially since the end of the Second World War, the people
who run corporations have come to understand that they
need good people as much as the good people need the
corporations. The result has been a dramatic shift in the
balance of power between employees and employers, and
a stunning improvement in the lives of and opportunities available to Corporate World employees in the United
States and in most other Western countries.

The result is that if you are competent and effective,
working in the Corporate World today can be, compared
to the alternatives of working for yourself, a low-stress,
relatively secure, intellectually interesting, and socially
rewarding way to earn a living.

LIFE IN THE CORPORATE WORLD

Let's look at life in today's Corporate World. Let's say
you've just graduated from college and you've found your
first job. Okay, stop right there.

Here you are with no business experience, and some
organization is going to pay you to work for it. You don't
have to make any financial investment, spend five to seven
years as an abused apprentice, or become an indentured
servant for seven to fifteen years. You don't need to have
any good ideas you can hopefully commercialize but that
in reality have a ten times greater likelihood of leading

you to bankruptcy than to success in your own business. All you have to do is make it through a few interviews and then show up for work. In a historical context, this is amazing indeed.

But the wonder doesn't end here. You may not be guaranteed a job or a pension, but as long as you're working for the company that hired you, you're going to get paid. It doesn't matter how badly the company does, how much money it loses, or even if it goes bankrupt. You still get paid. It's the law. If you're under the weather, having a bad week, or just not on your game for a while, you still get paid. If you're ill and can't come in to work for a few days or even a week or month, you still get paid. You even get paid when you go on vacation.

Too many people don't understand how unusual all this is. In the old days, before employees became as important to corporations as corporations were to employees, if you had a bad day, or if you were ill, or if you wanted to take a vacation, you could be summarily fired and replaced with another person desperate for your job.

Compare this to being a true entrepreneur. If you're running your own business and it's not making money, you don't make any money. None. Zero. Maybe you even have to take whatever savings you have and put it into the business to be sure the people who work for you get paid.

Most small to medium-size entrepreneurial businesses require an almost superhuman, unrelenting attention to detail that doesn't allow for many bad days, sick days, or vacations. Few entrepreneurs can separate their business lives from their personal lives, get in the car at the end of the day, and put it all behind them until the next day or until after the weekend. None can simply leave for a new job if things are going badly or they're not making the progress they think they should be making. Life as part of the Corporate World can be far less stressful.

But none of these recent Corporate World advantages would be nearly as attractive if there weren't the potential for achieving financial independence working for someone else. The fact is that today it is possible to earn as much working for a company you don't own as all but the most successful business owners can earn with their own businesses. You just have to manage your career using this book's seven strategies so you stay on the fast earnings track and avoid the deadly eddies that capture so many Corporate World people.

THE BOTTOM LINE

The purpose of this discussion is not to disparage entrepreneurship and business ownership. Indeed, it's the spirit of entrepreneurship and risk taking that has largely been responsible for creating the businesses that make up the Corporate World in the United States. Instead, the purpose is to make a more balanced case for working in the Corporate World, an option whose attractiveness has greatly improved over the past several decades, but which still suffers bad press and which remains an inviting target for *Dilbert* cartoons and late-night talk show hosts.

Today there may be less security and more uncertainty in working for a large corporation than there was fifty years ago, but there is also far more potential, more flexibility, more intellectual interest, more opportunity for creativity, and far, far greater earnings potential. People who must start their own business will, and should, continue to do so. But today the realistic chance for an average above-average person in the Corporate World to become an Outstanding Success is far greater than if that same person becomes an entrepreneur and starts his or her own business.

The biggest problem with working in the Corporate World is that it has become so easy to just get by, to make good money for years and be comfortable with little thought to actually managing your career. It's too easy to get lulled into a state of complacency and false security and to waste valuable years of your life doing stuff that by midcareer leads down a black hole from which you cannot extricate yourself. It may not be as difficult to become an Outstanding Success working in the Corporate World as it is being an entrepreneur, but you must still take control of your career and your life.

In the course of writing this book, I have had the opportunity to discuss its ideas with many people. Some were businesspeople who had achieved Outstanding Success or were well on their way to achieving it. A few were people I coached in their careers, mostly people in phases II and III who needed a little help to get unstuck or otherwise move toward achieving Outstanding Success. Many others were students in their final year of college or graduate school to whom I spoke as a group. The one constant was that the book's strategies always raised practical questions.

I tried to address most of the questions in the body of the book, but a few continued to surface no matter what I wrote. I've kept track of the most important of these questions and addressed them in the last chapter. I hope questions you have are included among them. If they are not, e-mail me at gene@genebedell.com, and I'll try my best to respond.

CHAPTER 12

QUESTIONS NOT ASKED
FREQUENTLY ENOUGH

In this chapter, answers to such interesting career questions as:

- Why you shouldn't count on your boss to make you successful,

- Whether the seven Outstanding Success strategies work if you're a woman trying to balance career and family life, and

- Is Tony Soprano an Outstanding Success?

Questions are never indiscreet.
Answers sometimes are.

OSCAR WILDE

A REAL-WORLD
REALITY CHECK

While it isn't easy writing a book—certainly for me it isn't—at least I get to control the setting, circumstances, and assumptions the reader has to deal with. A career in the real world is never so accommodating. As we said in chapter 9, there are the irksome realities of bosses who are jerks, organizations that don't treat people fairly, prejudice, glass ceilings, emotional pressures to spend more time parenting, dead-end jobs, and so forth.

Of course I drew heavily from the experiences of my own career and the careers of the people I've worked with in writing the book to address some of these issues, but that's still going only as deep as one degree of separation. Fortunately, I have had the opportunity to share the book's strategies and advice with people whose backgrounds and experiences were entirely separate from mine. Some were students just about to start their careers, others were people in each of the four phases of their career, and some were people who had already achieved Outstanding Success. In every case, I worked to incorporate what I learned from their personal experiences and from their questions into the book.

As part of this real-world reality check, I was asked a number of questions I thought were particularly insightful or important. This chapter summarizes those I felt best articulated concerns shared by others. We'll start with what is probably the question I've received most often.

Isn't it enough just to be happy?
It's a wonderful thing to love your work and be truly happy

in your career. What more can anyone ask? As it turns out, a lot.

After reviewing an early draft of this book, a friend questioned the definition of Outstanding Success. He asked me to consider the hypothetical case of a struggling musician living near the poverty level who loves his work and who has no personal desire or need for more than the small amount of money he's now earning.

Here is a person who loves getting up in the morning and is passionate about his work. Because his needs are simple, he has no unfilled material needs. If asked, this person would say he's an Outstanding Success. Don't I agree?

The answer is no. I agree this person is happy, and that's certainly a good thing. In fact, in my view, it's a far, far better thing than being financially successful and not being happy. But being happy is not the same as being an Outstanding Success as we've defined it. Consider the following.

Imagine that you have three neighbors, all of whom are musicians. All are passionate about and love their work. They are all extraordinarily happy. The first is the man my friend described—a musician living at the poverty level who will retire poor, happy, and without leaving a mark on his field. The second also lives at the poverty level, but his innovative approach to music is breaking new ground. His work will influence the work of musicians for decades. The third also loves her work, but earns a seven-figure income every year writing scores for movies and television.

The second neighbor is happy and has achieved a marked influence on his field. That makes him an Outstanding Success. The third is happy and is a top 1% earner. That makes her an Outstanding Success. The first neighbor is happy but has had neither influence on his field nor high earnings. That makes him happy but not an Outstanding Success.

It's not that happiness is unimportant. It's so important that happy people consider themselves to be outstanding successes just by virtue of being happy with their work. Which is why I've defined Outstanding Success (capitalized) as different from what some people would consider to be outstanding success (not capitalized).

Take this one step further. Say our happy, financially strapped, but satisfied neighbor was not a musician. Instead let's say he was a PhD with low aspirations and material desires who was as happy as could be driving an ice cream truck. Worse still, what if it was recreational drugs that made this person happy? No one would classify such a person as an outstanding success, much less an Outstanding Success just because he was happy with his life. The fact that a person is happy playing music instead of driving an ice cream truck or taking recreational drugs isn't enough to change that. Clearly, merely being happy is not Outstanding Success.

How can a person with an unhappy personal life or miserable family life be considered an Outstanding Success?
This is a natural question because people who spend too much of their time, energy, and attention on their careers sometimes have little left over for anything else, including their families. But again, the answer comes back to the definition of Outstanding Success. Outstanding Success (capitalized) refers only to career success. So, yes, it is entirely possible for someone who has achieved Outstanding Success in his or her career to be an outstanding failure in life in general.

How to become an outstanding success raising your children, in your relationship with your spouse or significant other, or in life generally are subjects of a different book, one I am not so presumptuous to believe I can write. But my personal advice would be to set goals for your personal and career lives that are not incompatible. For example, it may not be possible to become an Outstanding Success at work and still be home by six for dinner with your family every night. But perhaps you can set a goal of being home for a sit-down family dinner three or four times a week, even if dinner on those weekday nights is served at eight o'clock.

Setting rules and goals for your family life (e.g., either my spouse or I will review our children's homework every day) and personal life (e.g., I will run four times a week) compartmentalizes your career and stops it from taking over the rest of your life. Take these family and personal goals as seriously as you do your career goals, and there should be an adequate balance between your career, your family, and whatever else is important to you. Then use the book's seven strategies for managing your career, and if you screw up the rest of your life, at least you can't blame your work.

Given your definition of Outstanding Success, would you say Tony Soprano and Jeff Skilling, the leader of Enron, were Outstanding Successes, at least until their downfall?

Tony Soprano, the fictional mob boss of the hit TV show *The Sopranos*, is, of course, not a real person. But on TV, at least before the series' last season, he certainly seemed happy with his work, albeit somewhat stressed by the inconvenient fact that someone might kill him at any moment. (Every occupation, I suppose, has its downside.)

Jeff Skilling, on the other hand, is very real, and although I have read several books about the Enron debacle, I cannot attest to Skilling's happiness. But the spirit of the question is: Tony Soprano was a top 1% earner, and Jeff Skilling was for many years both a top 1% earner and enormously influential in business. Assuming both were happy in their careers, would you consider them to have achieved Outstanding Success?

Again, it goes to definition. We must ignore the inconvenient facts that Tony Soprano doesn't exist and Skilling ruined the lives of loyal employees working for him and was convicted of numerous felonies. Assuming both were happy as crime boss and greedy CEO, both Tony Soprano and Jeff Skilling achieved Outstanding Success, for a time, in their reprehensible careers, even though no reasonable person believes they achieved outstanding success in their lives generally.

It is easy to dismiss this question as frivolous, but it isn't, because it goes to a fundamental principle. And that is, we are not here to judge career choices, just to help you become successful in whatever career choice you make. Of course, careers as crime boss and white-collar criminal are immoral. But that is the topic for a different discussion.

Whether you decide to become a teacher, marine, business executive, religious leader, lawyer, doctor, butcher, baker, or candlestick maker is up to you. You get to decide whether you work for a company that sells cancer cures or cigarettes, police radar units or radar detectors, infant formula or junk food. We can argue the value of a lifework, and we can discuss how to be most successful at one's chosen lifework. But Outstanding Success deals only with the latter.

Doesn't loyalty count for anything?

It is troubling to some people that the book's career strategies do not encourage loyalty—not to the organization you work for, nor to the people you work with. It does not, however, discourage friendship, which is important to distinguish from loyalty.

Loyalty is a feeling of devotion, duty, or attachment to something or someone. You can be loyal to your country, your alma mater, the company you work for, or the company that picks up your trash. You can also feel loyalty to your boss or to people who work for you.

Friendship, on the other hand, is a relationship between individuals (it makes no sense for an individual to be friends with an organization) that is characterized by mutual assistance, approval, and support. In my mind, a key aspect of friendship is that this mutual assistance, approval, and support transcend convenience.

If you wish to feel loyal to the organization you work for and the people you work with, that's certainly your prerogative. But you must accept the reality that the organization is not your friend, and the people you work with may not be true friends either. You may like, depend on, and support one another, but that is not the same as true friendship, because in the end, it's almost certain that the organization you work for and the people you work with will take actions in their best interests, not in yours.

They will move the plant to Mexico, relocate headquarters halfway across the country even though your children are in the middle of their junior year in high school, or consolidate school districts and eliminate the one you've been teaching in for twenty-five years. A star employee you've been grooming or the boss you've come to depend on will move to another job if the opportunity arises. As well they should. Be as loyal as you feel you want to be, but do it knowing that your loyalty may not be reciprocated and may cost you dearly.

Is this too cynical a worldview? Consider that few organizations inspire more loyalty than the U.S. Marine Corps. But if you're wounded in action and are unable to serve, you'll soon find yourself discharged. If you're an officer committed to the corps but you don't get promoted according to a predetermined schedule, they discharge you. (The Marine Corps, like New York City law firms and many other good organizations, has an up-or-out policy.)

No, the Marine Corps is not your friend, no matter how much you love it and no matter how loyal to it you are. That is not a slur against the Marine Corps, an organization I deeply respect and in which my daughter is an officer. It is reality. And if we should expect the Marine Corps to act in its best interests, what can you expect of any other organization?

Friendship, on the other hand, is an entirely different issue. Friends are people you can count on through thick and thin and who should be able to count on you through thick and thin. Friends are far more important than organizations and short-term career considerations. The Marine Corps may discharge you if you are physically unfit to serve, but individual marines will risk their lives to save fellow marines.

I have said plainly that a key success strategy is to treat the organization you work for as if you owned it. Nevertheless, I would never fire a friend who happened to be working for me because it was in the best interests of the organization. I learned this the hard way.

Based on his deteriorating performance and erratic behavior and at the urging of my entire management team, I once fired someone who in the course of working for me had become a true friend. I put the needs of the company I worked for ahead of my friend's needs, and I consider it one of the biggest mistakes of my career. The company passed through my life as companies tend to do, but in the meantime I permanently lost a good friend.

So, regarding loyalty to the organization, there is no softening. As we said in chapter 6, the organization you work for has no feelings or needs. It is a legal construct. Moreover, even if you see the organization as the people who work for it, evidence shows that loyalty among bosses and employees generally persists only so long as it is to everyone's mutual benefit. Be judicious with how you spend career assets and what career options you forgo for loyalty. True friendship, on the other hand, is worth a very high cost indeed.

Don't some businesses have a higher purpose than simply making money?

No. Of course there are many residual benefits, e.g., better living through chemistry, and residual costs, e.g., lung cancer from cigarettes, that are the consequences of a business's primary purpose of making money. But whatever good a business does is no more its raison d'être than causing lung cancer is the raison d'être of the tobacco companies. Aside from making money, all else is a consequence, either good or bad, intended or unintended.

So beware of anyone in business who is sitting on some higher moral horse. You can bet he lives in a bigger house, has a way bigger boat, and is probably trying to get you to do something not entirely in your best interests. He is being disingenuous at best, dishonest at worst, or is deluded and not someone you can safely trust to make the organization successful.

Won't it look bad if I change jobs too frequently?

Whether frequent job changes count against you depends largely on what you accomplished at your past jobs, why you changed jobs, and your age. If you have a clearly demonstrable record of consistently delivering Outstanding Performance, your record of job changes has to be extreme and the reasons arbitrary for it to count seriously against you. But since it typically takes time to position yourself so you can deliver Outstanding Performance, it is unlikely you will be able to do so over an extended period and still change jobs so frequently that it becomes an issue. Focus on delivering Outstanding Performance in every job you have and the rest will take care of itself.

It can happen, however, that despite your best efforts, your job doesn't allow you to deliver Outstanding Performance or work in your Outstanding Success Zone. If that happens early in your career, people understand. You're searching, looking for your right place. But the longer the searching goes on and the more jobs you move through in a short time, the more people start to believe that perhaps there is no right place for you.

So don't be afraid to change jobs if you're not in your Outstanding Success Zone or your job doesn't allow you to deliver Outstanding Performance. But at some point, you've got to settle down and prove you can deliver Outstanding Performance.

My boss is incompetent (is a jerk, doesn't like me, isn't someone I respect, doesn't know how to manage people,

doesn't know I exist, isn't a good manager, is out for himself, doesn't appreciate my contribution, plays favorites, etc. Choose as many as you like or add your own boss outrages). How can I deliver Outstanding Performance or achieve Outstanding Success working for someone like this?

This question demonstrates a fundamental misunderstanding of the relationship between people and their bosses. Most people believe it's up to their boss to help them become successful, and consequently, they give their boss too important a role in their own success. Thinking this way puts someone else—the random person you happen to be working for at the moment—in charge of your destiny.

Hopefully, though not necessarily, you will have a few wonderful bosses who will help you succeed (and if you want to become an Outstanding Success, you should be a boss who helps the people who work for you succeed). But you can be pretty well assured that over the course of a forty-year career, you will also have many more bosses who will provide you no help whatsoever unless you lead the way.

Once you accept this fact of organizational life, you'll be far less concerned with whom you work for. Of course you want to work for a supportive, reasonably intelligent boss who has the organization's best interests at heart, but competence, leadership, and management excellence aren't necessary. They aren't necessary, because *your boss's job isn't to make you successful. It's your job to make your boss successful.*

It doesn't matter if you don't like your boss or if she's incompetent or a bad manager. When you make your boss successful, which you do by applying the strategies in this book, you will be amazed at how much better a boss the person you work for will become. Suddenly her competence isn't key to your success—only your competence matters. How well she manages you is irrelevant because you're managing yourself and you're managing her. Unless your boss is entirely dysfunctional, you will win her attention, support, and encouragement, because people automatically pay attention to, support, and encourage whatever makes them successful.

With this said, we have to accept that occasionally you might work for a boss whose actions or management style truly prevent you from delivering Outstanding Performance or from working in your Outstanding Success Zone. If that's really the case, and you believe you'll be stuck working for this person for a long time, you have to change jobs, either by transferring to a different part of the organization you now work for or changing organizations completely.

But be careful before you come to this conclusion. It's too easy to blame your boss for whatever problems you're having. As long as the person you work for supports you, which is little to ask given you're out to make her successful—your success depends on you and the people who work for you, not on your boss.

What if it's impossible to deliver Outstanding Performance in my job?

When someone tells me there's nothing they can do that would be considered Outstanding Performance, the first question I ask is: "Are you sure, or is it that you haven't studied the organization well enough to figure out what it is you can do to deliver Outstanding Performance?"

I ask this because I've found that most people don't understand that they usually have much more control over their destinies than they believe. But they have to take the initiative and go beyond their job description to discover how they can deliver Outstanding Performance. Too often, they just look to their boss or their job description to tell them what they should be doing and how to become successful.

That being said, there are also many situations where a person's job and career opportunities are limited by the boundaries of their job description. For example, Daniel was an attorney working for a company's legal staff and was assigned to work full-time helping the company's IT department negotiate legal agreements with suppliers. Daniel's assignment was to prevent the IT department from committing any legal blunders, and there was nothing he could do that would be considered Outstanding Performance.

There are many such support, impossible-to-deliver-Outstanding-Performance jobs, especially in large organizations. If there's truly nothing you can do that would be considered Outstanding Performance, then you must change jobs or even organizations. No matter how well you do your job, and no matter how much people reward you with accolades and excellent performance reviews, you will not achieve Outstanding Success.

I am a minority (or a woman). Do the strategies really work if you're a not a male white Anglo-Saxon Protestant?

Emphatically yes, if you're working for an organization that's worth working for. This answer recognizes that prejudice, both illegal and legal, still exists. (An example of legal prejudice might be a prejudice against people without an Ivy League education, or without an engineering degree, or against people who did not begin their career in sales, or any number of preconceived notions that will hold you back. While these do not rise to the level of odiousness as a prejudice against race, gender, or religion, they can be equally detrimental to career advancement in some organizations.) You have two choices when you encounter prejudice you believe is holding you back—fight or flight.

There are two ways to fight—for retribution or for recognition. People choose to fight for retribution when they believe a wrong has been done to them. The fight plays out in the courts, and success is financial compensation for the wrong.

This kind of fight is everyone's right, but it is not the kind of after-the-fact fight we're talking about here. While success in a fight for retribution may help balance the result of illegal prejudice, and fighting in this way may be the only path to change and justice in some organizations, it is not the type of fight that will lead to Outstanding Success. It will lead to years of turmoil, uncertainty, and career distraction. But if it's something you feel you have to do to set things right, then follow your heart. But know that while your fight may help right a wrong, it is not likely to help you achieve Outstanding Success in your career.

The fight that may both right a wrong and help you achieve Outstanding Success takes place in the offending organization, not in the courts. It may not be easy, but someone has to be the first woman partner, the first African-American senior executive in your firm, the next person of your faith to crack the glass ceiling. It might as well be you. This is often a difficult, perhaps uncomfortable, and lonely fight to take on, and you may have to work especially hard to gain the recognition you deserve. But if you feel it is a fight you're willing to undertake and that it's ultimately winnable given the nature of the organization you work for, the strategies for Outstanding Success are the seven strategies set out in this book.

It may happen, however, that you do not feel the prize is worth the effort, or that the prejudice is so ingrained in the organization that there is little likelihood you will succeed no matter what you do. It is entirely reasonable, then, to leave the fight for someone else and move on to an environment where you are accepted and it is possible for you to achieve Outstanding Success without first having to fight social injustice. This is the flight option.

Pick the fights that stir your passions and that are so personally meaningful to you that they're worthy of whatever sacrifice is required along the way. Move on from all others that will only merely make you angry and ultimately hold you back and cause you to waste time and energy.

Can these strategies work for a woman who values time with her children and a genuine work-life balance?

Of course this same question can be asked by men seeking work-life balance, but in point of fact, it is only women who have asked it of me.

Referring to a dynamic career and a full and satisfying personal life, someone once said, "You can have it all. But you can't have it all at the same time." No matter how smart you are or how hard you're willing to work, it is a fact of nature that every week has only 168 hours. Subtract the time used for sleeping, eating, grooming, and other miscellaneous personal overhead, and for most people this 168 hours is reduced to fewer than 100 hours.

Both men and women have to decide how much of this hundred hours they want to devote to their careers and how much to children, significant others, and non-work personal life activities. How happy, healthy, wealthy, rested, and fulfilled you will be, not just with your work but with your entire life, will depend in large part in how you choose to use these hundred hours every week.

There are time robbers that steal from these hundred hours without contributing meaningfully to either your work or your personal happiness—commuting, business travel, watching television, useless meetings. Then there's the life overhead of shopping, cleaning, cutting the grass, paying the bills, walking the dog, ferrying the kids to play-dates and soccer, and so forth.

Both men and women face these same physical realities, but in Western societies at least, more often than not they face them with different pressures and needs. For whatever reason, whether due to social pressure, relationship dynamics, parental expectations, or biology, the average mother will want to or be forced to allocate more of her hundred hours to raising children than will the average father. To exacerbate the problem, let's be honest here, men, most of us are not very good at doing our share of the household overhead.

The result is that the average mother in a two-career household with children finds herself trying to squeeze too many hours of stuff into her hundred-hour sack. Add to this the guilt women often feel if they believe they're shortchanging their children (whether they in fact are is beside the point), and it's not surprising that neither work nor personal life provides the joy to women in two-career households that they could in less stressed circumstances. It's even worse for single mothers.

So the answer to the question is that the seven strategies will work just as effectively for anyone, including both parties in a two-career family with children. The issue isn't work strategies but the management of the couple's time, domestic duties, and values.

If both parties feel that at least one parent must always be with the children in their early years and that domestic help is not an acceptable or affordable option, and if both parents are pursuing time-intensive careers that require long commutes, late hours, and extensive travel, then no, the strategies will not work.

But the issue is not with the strategies, but with the failure to accept the need to make realistic choices regarding the allocation of each partner's hundred hours. Make choices that use more than the couple's combined two hundred hours, or more than a hundred of one of the partner's hours, and trouble's brewing—stress, conflict, disappointment, guilt, recriminations.

Choose a life strategy first, and accept that the benefits of your choice always come with a cost paid in lost options and opportunities. Then focus on managing your career with the book's seven strategies to make the best of whatever time you've chosen to allocate to your career.

How do I decide what organization to work for?

You always want to work for an organization that makes it possible for you to deliver Outstanding Performance and work in your Outstanding Success Zone. We've gone over that at length in the book. But there are other considerations as well.

First, a rising tide raises all ships, and if earnings potential is important to you, you should first target an industry and a company that is profitable, preferably growing, and where others in the company have high earnings. If you are an outstanding performer in a company that's struggling and where even the most senior people have modest earnings, you are unlikely to be rewarded adequately for your efforts no matter how outstanding they may be.

The exception to this is the turnaround, where a management team is brought in to fix a moribund or failing organization. Know, however, that this is a higher-risk career option than joining a successful company. Of course there are many situations where a competent management team has saved a struggling organization, but far more failing organizations have passed the point where leadership and good management can turn them around. Past mistakes, market forces, political blunders, or advancing technology have put them in positions of weakness that are, if not inevitably fatal, fatal enough to reduce them forever to the role of struggling hanger-on.

If you're intrigued by the challenges and opportunities of being part of a turnaround, go for it. But do so knowing that your probability of achieving Outstanding Success, even if you deliver Outstanding Performance, is lower than if you join an organization in its ascendancy.

Apart from the success of the industry or organization you're joining, you should also try to target an organization where you fit in—where the culture is consistent with your background, personality, and beliefs. Outstanding Performance may win out over all, but you must accept the reality that people are more likely to promote and reward those with whom they feel most comfortable.

This cultural compatibility is not a necessity; indeed, it may sometimes not be possible. Lynn, who we mentioned in chapters 2 and 8, would never have become one of the first women partners in her New York law firm if she hadn't joined a firm that had never made a woman partner in its history. Greg, who we met briefly in chapter 9, would never have become the first CIO to be made a managing director of a leading Wall Street investment bank if he hadn't chosen to join a firm that had never made a managing director that didn't come from corporate finance or the trading floor.

Nevertheless, it is easier to become successful if you fall squarely within the culture of the people who decide who will become successful. Moreover, this comfort works both ways—it will be easy for you to fit in and enjoy working with like-minded people. Again, cultural fit is not a necessity for achieving Outstanding Success, but something you should factor into the equation if you have a choice. It's always easier and more enjoyable swimming with the current than against it.

What is the biggest mistake people make in their careers?

There are two big mistakes I see people make. The most common is failure to manage their careers. They manage their finances, manage their relationships, manage every aspect of their children's upbringing, manage their departments, even manage their companies, but never give a thought to the idea that their forty-year career is one of the most important things of all to manage. Intelligent, hard-working, driven people go to work day after day, occasionally changing jobs in response to unexpected turmoil or opportunities, but do not manage their careers with the same unwavering tenacity and purpose they bring to the rest of their lives.

It's easy to understand how people can make this mistake. Most jobs come with promotions, raises, and recognition, especially during the first ten to twenty years. All this positive feedback serves to divert your attention elsewhere in your life. After all, your career is taking care of itself nicely, thank you. Of course it isn't, but people can be fooled into thinking it is.

It's the big second mistake people make that is much less easy to understand. It is people's failure to act once they know their career is not going where they had hoped. The certain knowledge that things aren't going well will typically happen suddenly, perhaps in response to some specific event, say, a failure to win a promotion, the first time the annual wage increase is far less than expected, being assigned to report to a younger manager, seeing colleagues move ahead, or simply waking up one morning and realizing it's no longer fun to go to work. But whatever the precipitating event, there it is in full clarity for the first time—"I'm not happy, and this career isn't going where I want it to go." Bummer. But if you act soon after you first realize there's a problem, it's usually not too late to fix things.

Except that people don't act, even when they know there's a problem and even when they know what to do. The big mistake is that people just persevere in their jobs, unwilling to make changes for fear that—well, for fear of all sorts of things. Fear that, although this may not be the career they wanted, perhaps this is the best of all possible career worlds and any change might even be worse. Or the fear of giving up the security they have or the paycheck that's coming in. Or the fear of disrupting the family. Or simply the fear of admitting a failure. So they go on until the roof caves in and they're fired or otherwise lose their jobs. Or they stick it out until retirement, unhappy for the last ten to twenty years of their careers.

The time to manage your career is always. The time to make important career changes is immediately when you first realize you're unhappy or your career is not taking you where you want to go. Not managing your career at all times and failing to make changes when it's clear changes are necessary are the two biggest career mistakes you can make. It may be scary to make a change and face the prospect of making a mistake. But failure to take action and living with a mistake for years, even decades, is the scariest of all.

We've come to the end. All of the 99% of people who are not now achieving Outstanding Success in their careers can dramatically increase their level of success by following the book's seven strategies. Many can achieve Outstanding Success and become top 1% earners or influencers. All that's needed is the courage to tenaciously manage your career and make the changes that open the way to Outstanding Success. You're in control. Take over.

ACKNOWLEDGMENTS

Thank You

I've known I wanted to be a writer since I was in grade school. I still have stories I wrote when I was very young, which I occasionally look at when I want to embarrass myself. But by high school, I also knew I didn't want to spend my life serving hamburgers while I paid my dues and established myself as an author. So I took the coward's way out and went into engineering and then business so I could afford the sports cars, apartments, and, eventually, family that would have been a challenge on the earnings of a struggling writer.

That was, as it happens, a prescient decision, because I turned out to be considerably better at business than at writing. This last fact I learned while writing my first book in 1985.

Writing a good nonfiction book requires that you have something important to say, that you have an engaging voice to say it in, and that you're well grounded in the mechanics of writing. I naively thought I was an ace in all three departments, an illusion I was disabused of when I asked friends and colleagues to read my stuff. That is when I learned that, at least for me, there is a fourth requirement for writing a good nonfiction book—friends, agents, and editors who have the patience to read early drafts and tell me honestly what they think.

Having reviewed early manuscripts for others, I can provide personal evidence that this can rank right up there with cleaning out the garage as a fun way to spend your time. Nevertheless, I have been fortunate to have many people willing to read and comment on the ideas and writing in this book as it developed, and discuss it with me at length. A few words at the end of a book and a free copy are hardly adequate thanks for their attention, patience, and efforts, but here goes.

I am especially grateful to Laureen Bedell, Barry Libenson, Tom Dungan, and Jay Graves for their meticulous reading of the manuscript and discussing the ideas with me at length. Laureen Bedell and Tom Dungan actually had the interest and patience to read multiple drafts as the work developed.

I am also grateful to Jay Gaines, Dennis McKinnie, Jose Rodriguez, Captain Chris Timms, and Srini Vasan for their comments and suggestions, and to Vivek Wadhwa and Jeff Glass for making it possible for me to present the book's concepts to several hundred Duke University graduate engineering students over several years. The students' reactions were important in helping me judge how people at the very beginning of their careers would react to the idea of becoming wealthy as well as happy, and to gauge how receptive they would be to doing what is required to achieve the two together.

There's a special thank you to Susan Leahey, my partner in executive coaching. Her years of hands-on coaching experience with people in all walks of life gave me a perspective that influenced the presentation as well as the ideas.

I'm not sure whether to thank or apologize to my children, Zoe and Zachary. First, they had to endure innumerable car rides stuck listening to me try out ideas. (It is lucky all my cars have automatic door locks.) But it was more than the torment of having to listen to me. Zoe is a

U.S. Marine officer and Zachary a rock musician, which pretty much brackets all possible career options, and they unwittingly provided me a constant supply of their friends on whom I could try out ideas and approaches. These conversations with their friends and with the students I met at Duke University led me to understand that young people full of potential and facing no apparent career challenges needed Outstanding Success career guidance almost more than midcareer men and women struggling with immediate career issues.

I am especially fortunate to be represented by literary agents Glen Hartley and Lynn Chu at Writers Representatives and to have the support and guidance of the professionals at HarperCollins. These people include Ethan Friedman, Sarah Brown, Amy Vreeland, and Anne Greenberg.

There is a special thanks to all the people (and I hope you don't know who you are) whose stories I used throughout the book. Some achieved Outstanding Success and some did not. In any case, I worked hard to disguise their identities by changing not just their names, lines of work, and occasionally their genders, but also the unimportant identifying facts behind their stories. So if you're a friend and you think you recognize yourself in a story, you're probably wrong. You're in another story that doesn't seem like you at all.

Finally, I again thank my wife, Deborah. She helped me with this book as she helped me with my previous books. But far more importantly, she helped me find happiness in my personal life that made it so much easier to find happiness in my career. And for this I am grateful beyond words.

About the Author

Gene Bedell began his career as an instructor in the school of engineering and science at New York University, but after three years of earning $5,750 a year, concluded that teaching at a university was unlikely to lead to achieving Outstanding Success. What followed was a career in business that included stints in marketing, sales, corporate finance, manufacturing, consulting, information technology, and general management.

He has been a senior executive and board member of very small businesses and very large ones, of public companies and of private ones. His experiences range from working in Dakota City, Nebraska, as general manager of the country's largest beef processor, to working on Wall Street, where he was a partner in one of the world's leading investment banks. He founded three businesses, one of which he took public and grew to sales of more than $117 million in five years. He was named an Entrepreneur of the Year in North Carolina for emerging growth companies.

He currently spends his time writing, doing career coaching to help others try to achieve Outstanding Success, public speaking, and playing squash. He can be reached by e-mail at gene@genebedell.com.